GET A JOB

Other guides by Jack van Minden
published by Management Books 2000

All About Psychological Tests and Assessment Centres
Headhunters
The IQ Trainer
Selection Interviews
The Ultimate Guide to Salary Negotiation

For a complete list of Management Books 2000 titles
visit our web-site on http://www.mb2000.com

GET A JOB

Jack van Minden

Based on the Dutch book "Get a Job" by Jack van Minden, published in the Netherlands in 2009 by Business Contacts

This adapted UK version first published in 2011 by Management Books 2000 Ltd
Forge House, Limes Road
Kemble, Cirencester
Gloucestershire, GL7 6AD, UK
Tel: 0044 (0) 1285 771441
Fax: 0044 (0) 1285 771055
Email: info@mb2000.com
Web: www.mb2000.com

British Library Cataloguing in Publication Data is available

ISBN 9781852526511

Dedicated to Bep and Dé,

for they have known the real hard times.

CONTENTS

Introduction 9

1 Assertive Jobhunting 13

2 Knowing: 27
   Who You Are, What You Can Do and What You Want

3 Investigate: 59
   Where Are Those Jobs?

4 React: 89
   Write, Call and Mail

5 Administer: 117
   Making and Managing Lists

6 Prepare: 127
   *Research the Employers, Their Jobs and Go for the
   Interview*

7 Carry Out: 145
   Interviews and Assessments

8 Sign the Contract: 171
   Negotiating the Best Salaries and Benefits

Useful Websites 187

Index 189

INTRODUCTION

Life would be so beautiful and easy if there where tens of employers waiting on the sidewalk for you, praying and begging and pleading with you to come to work for them.

Wake up! Those good old times have passed. Perhaps they will return, but that does not do you any good now. When employers are kicking out (all) their employees before they are taking on new personnel, then you have a problem. This book helps you to keep your head clear, so that you can tackle this problem quickly, systematically and effectively, by continually taking the correct steps. We will guard you against the many traps and dangers that beset the jobhunting process, and we will offer lots of advice and tricks (in the form of tips), so you can achieve positive results.

These are difficult times. There are fewer vacancies than we have been used to in the past. (But hey, employers are not obliged to please you!) The less educated (cheap labour) are pushing out the higher educated – what will that lead to? We will not delve into these kinds of important issues, since we are concerned with the present, not the future – how to get a job *now*.

A job application is a test – one of many in your life. After reading this book, you will easily sail through this 'proof of competency'. You will learn to manage yourself better, which is a lot more difficult than managing your possible future subordinates!

We strongly suggest you spend one part of **each** day jobhunting. What do you do during that time, now more than ever before? You spend the time –

- *thinking* about what you want from a (next) job and – in the long term – how you can give your career a boost;
- *reading*, for example which suitable vacancies are 'in stock';
- *phoning*, finding out more about a position, networking or to 'selling' yourself to employers;

- *applying* for a job that appeals to you;
- *travelling* to the employer or the intermediary;
- *talking*, for example during a job or selection interview;
- *thinking of* which answers you will give during a personality test;
- *formulating* what you want to earn when hired.

This book deals with the complete jobhunting process, from the very beginning (what do I want?), all the way through to the signing of the contract with the employer. It will help you develop a strategic approach and, step by step, to find and consider relevant job vacancies, put together a CV, carry out research on employers that you want to investigate, make your application, prepare yourself for job interviews, improve your performance during the assessments, acquire a higher salary (and everything which is associated with it), and much more. Naturally, the many tips and tricks are also applicable when the labour market starts picking up.

What is important when looking for a job during difficult times, is that you are just that little bit **smarter** than the hoards of other jobhunters. We will help you with this, by giving you many tried and tested techniques, so that you end up in pole position – because you don't have much use for a silver or bronze medal when only the gold counts. This book will prove its worth for jobhunters, as well as starters and people re-entering the job market.

Get a Job! will not create jobs, but it will help you improve your (starting) position in relation to the many hungry competitors. You will become more resilient and – also important – flexible. Look at it as the helpdesk that can finally offer real solutions.

All it will cost you is a little time – but keep in mind: the more you invest in the jobhunting process, the more chances you will create to destroy the invisible competition. Grab a hold of the many weapons in this book! Take charge! The methods that are described are proven recipes. We at Psycom have been working for tens of years applying them and have helped generations of jobhunters find suitable, pleasurable and well paying work (or start their own business).

Many points in *Get a Job!* will be only touched on or briefly described, so that you can start looking for a job at turbo speed right away. Every chapter stands alone. You do not have to read the book in one breath and in one sitting. Do you want to know more about a certain topic? You can find more about that subject in one or more of my other career books.

Learning is a two-way process. All our clients have learned from us, but we have also learned a lot from them. 'Maybe it is a stupid question...' often leads to new thoughts and insights. We would like to thank all Psycom business contacts for sharing their problems, questions and suggestions. They have laid – without realising it – the basis for writing this book.

Success is a choice!

1

ASSERTIVE JOBHUNTING

Your next job is **your** responsibility. It is a pity that during a recession those 'dream' jobs are barely attainable, and that, more than likely, you will be looking for an 'in-between job' where you can park yourself for as long as necessary. (If you manage to come across your dream job, that is even better!) But you always have choices – to take action or not, choose between job A or job B, be a manager or be managed, move for a job or stay where you are living. If you want to 'score', get a job, then you will need to make an effort, every single day. Only the sun comes up for free – but sometimes you have to make a trip to experience that. This book will help you create a plan to find a job during difficult economic times and put your plan into action. That will demand plenty of energy.

The threat of unemployment

Due to these turbulent times and the impact of globalisation, many jobs have been lost. Take for instance the disappearance of jobs during the meltdown of the financial sector in the credit crisis of 2008–2009, or the western auto industry where many companies went bankrupt or have only been kept solvent by generous government support.

In poor economic times many companies go 'belly up', and cost-cutting and reduced budgets are a fact of life – and that includes in non-commercial sectors. There are mergers and takeovers and services are outsourced. This all leads to redundancies since, in general, personnel costs are the biggest outlay – that is where companies can attain the most 'profit'. While the redundancy procedure is usually an impersonal, somewhat formal, procedure for the employer, many affected employees find themselves in a serious crisis, comparable with the death of a loved one or with emigration.

Of course, there are some unemployed people who wake up cheering: *Hurray! Another jolly and sunny day, free to do what I want.* Relaxation. No hassles with any boss. No irritating clients. No stress. And if they're lucky, a fat severance package making sure that any pain due to the redundancy was softened. And without that bulky envelope? Then you adjust your standard of living and find out how little money you actually need to get by. You can still make jokes about how you love working, especially watching other people doing it.

Many unemployed people see this period as a paid vacation. While it is true that you lose your work 'friends' (what kind of friends are those!), your loyal buddies are busy at work. Another problem: how do you fill up your time? You start asking yourself: Am I doing the right things? How come time seems to slip through my fingers? The paradox is: the more time you have available, the less you get done. (A wise lesson: if you need help with something, get it from a busy person, because that's that one who gets things done.) There can be a growing sense of social isolation: 'My days are empty, I can barely get out of bed – and why in heaven's name do I need to get up? I drag myself through the city, look at the shop windows, maybe I bump into an acquaintance. But that will probably not happen, because they are all working... I have nothing to do. Buying a postage stamp is the highlight of the day. Maybe there will be something exciting on television tonight.'

And what do you do about your high rent or mortgage now? You will feel a painful pressure. If the search for the desired job takes too long you may run out of unemployment benefits. That is not a pretty picture, since the cost of living remains the same. The difference between income and spending gets out of balance so that angry letters from banks, landlords and debt collectors start appearing in your letterbox on a daily basis. Why would you open those letters when you already have enough bad news? Not knowing seems better... Too bad that sticking your head in the sand only results in more problems. Time gnaws on like a rat. Another month goes by. You will have to work hard on looking for jobs if you want to avoid this downward spiral.

This book is aptly named *Get a Job!*, but for the reader who has given up a better title could be *Get a Life!* since unemployment makes many unemployed people feel depressed and defeated and leads to low energy and 'doing nothing'. The longer you are out of a job, the more difficult it is to get back in the swing of things. And you still have another thirty or forty years to go!

Employment in a permanent job makes most people feel useful, since they contribute to society. Their work challenges them daily, keeps them sharp, provides satisfaction and provides contacts and friends – and money. Even people who are financially secure, who don't *have* to work, find a paying job to be more attractive than a daily visit to the golf course.

TIP

Have you been fired without a clear cause? Don't look back, look ahead. What is behind you is finished. If you are still emotionally down and getting upset about every day, then you may be writing negatively tinted application letters and sitting at job interviews with clenched fists. That is definitely not how you want to present yourself.

Every crisis is also a chance

But it is not all that negative. When you are working for an employer where jobs keep disappearing, that does not necessarily mean that you will be the next victim. And this also applies when you work alone in a department that used to have five employees. Even in times of economic crisis there are always people who know how to improve their situation and prosper:

1. A competitor that leaves the sector or market (or is investing less), results in new possibilities for the remaining players, which will strengthen your chances to score.

2. You and/or your company can consider developing new products or services that will increase profits or cut costs for client-firms.

3. If many people have been shown the door in your company, its overhead will plummet and you will have to work harder while others will become more dependent on your efforts, experience, skills and knowledge. You can turn this into a pay raise during the next round of salary negotiations.

4. When colleagues with a company car are made redundant, the contract between the employer and lease company will probably hold. That means that your firm will have 'unused' cars which still carry their monthly costs. If you don't have a company car, it would be the right time to broach the subject with your boss... Do you want to increase the chance that it works? Offer to pay a monthly contribution. Then it will be more profitable for the company! And maybe you can get a good deal on an unused desk or office chair. One person's downfall is another person's victory.

5. A shrinking number of employees in your company may present you with the opportunity to (temporarily) take over the work from a redundant colleague. Maybe those are activities that you have always dreamt of doing, or that can help when changing careers, that you can add to your CV in any case. This is your golden chance to finally prove what you are worth and show your talents.

6. And when it gets too quiet in your department, offer your services to other departments. Get to know other people in the company. Perhaps the work will appeal to you so much that you want to put in a transfer!

7. Would this be the right moment to acquire options or shares in your company, now that the chips are down? (With or without the financial support of your employer.) You send a signal that you have confidence in the organisation, in yourself and in the long-term survival of the company. But if

you see the storm clouds approaching and your sheltered spot is threatened, then start looking for a new job.

Stay where you are

The strategy 'stay where you are and don't make waves' can be sensible during an economic malaise. Even more true, research shows that most employees do not consider changing jobs during these periods, to avoid taking unnecessary risks. But that means a stagnation in your career path (as well as your salary). This approach is not without danger, since you could be confronted with unexpected developments if you do not remain alert. For instance, bankruptcy or mergers could put an end to your job.

What is your position in your organisation? Do you have a unique talent? A shining track record? Are you irreplaceable? Or are you slowly being shown the exit? If threatened with redundancy, make a list of your achievements over the past year that you can present to your employer. This can also be used as ammunition for your future jobhunting.

During economically challenging times, many employers replace more expensive (older, experienced) employees with younger ones – bingo, cost savings! But the reality is that making someone redundant can be rather expensive. And further it costs the employer money (and time) to recruit, select, train and introduce the new employees to the company. In addition, it takes time before the recruit knows his way around and is finally productive. (And don't forget: newcomers always make beginner's mistakes.) That attractive saving may not look so advantageous after all... If it becomes necessary, you can always make your boss aware of this.

Difficult labour market, stiff competition

What is characteristic in times of economic downturn is that there are more jobseekers competing for less vacancies. During a crisis you have less choice. Luckily, it is never bad everywhere; there are always areas where life goes on as usual, such as the government, schools, healthcare and the defence sector. Non-profit organisations are thus desirable employers. Some business sectors are less exposed to recession than others, while there are some sectors doing booming business *because* of the economic crisis – for instance when the consumer chooses for a cheaper alternative (think about groceries and restaurants) or get into financial trouble (which is good for debt collectors). And if companies can no longer economise (which is easy to do in the beginning), they will resort to hiring sales employees to increase their turnover.

Even in difficult times, people find new jobs. But some people find it much tougher than others. Older folks have a disadvantage, since companies would rather hire cheaper employees. Part-timers, handicapped employees or people with particular cultural or religious needs find it harder to find a job. Employers will be less quick to honour these special needs – they have too much choice.

Can you put off the inevitable?

Some people think that jobhunting means endlessly writing letters, accumulating information about employers and interviews which translates into standing up, politely shaking hands and answering the same questions time and time again. There is nothing they hate doing more. When they realise this, it is no wonder they check out. This is not the smart thing to do. But people often do stupid things...

Even if you hate jobhunting and have faced rejection many times, the point is to keep going, because otherwise you will lose your touch. It will become more difficult to wake yourself up from your hibernation. The next generation of jobhunters is waiting in the wings. Giving up is not an option.

When is the best time to get started? **Now**! If you see a suitable vacancy, your first positive thought needs to be: I am going to get that job. Nowadays you need to be smarter and more creative than your competition.

Formulate your goals – make it a project

Formulate a number of concrete objectives for yourself. Then you will know what you have to focus on. For example, if you are looking for a job in the financial sector you might have the following goals:

- find employment before ……. (*specific date*) – with this goal in mind you can plan the preceding steps;
- a position with a bank or insurance company (or broader still: the financial sector);
- preferred position: client administrator (account manager or similar position);
- full-time (preferably 4 X 9);
- in the north of the country;
- desired salary (minimum): £50,000 + company car.

Turn it into a (short and effective) project. You do not have to be an out-of-control telephone salesperson, like the kind that annoy you at dinner-time, but be as active and alert as possible during your jobhunting project. You play a number of roles in this project, including the leader's.

Be careful that you do not fall into the film director's trap, who wrote the script and plays the starring role, and therefore produces a film that is way too long. He cannot bear to eliminate unnecessary scenes, because it is after all his creation. Hopefully, this will not happen to you as a 'project manager'. Remain critical.

Jobhunting is KIRAP-CS

The jobhunting procedure requires the following necessary steps:

- writing an application covering letter;
- putting together a CV;
- after receiving an invitation, attending a job interview;
- (sometimes) taking a pre-employment assessment test;
- negotiating an employment contract (or accepting right away).

The KIRAP-CS process for landing a job, which fits together like the gears of a cog, contains all the steps needed, from A to Z, with everything in-between to increase your chances for success. It is an acronym for the following words:

> **K**now,
> **I**nvestigate,
> **R**eact,
> **A**dminister,
> **P**repare,
> **C**arry out and,
> **S**ign the contract.

You put them together for the optimal combination; all the individual parts must be properly executed. And during the interview and assessment you will have to shine!

Seeing things from the employer's perspective

Most employers are looking for straight-laced men and women who have finished their education without a fuss, graduated and rolled from one job to the next. In other words, people without stains or dents, with a clear path straight up their career ladder, without surprises or irregularities – that's what bosses like to see! Chances are that you do not fulfil this ideal profile. Therefore, it is your job to adjust this distorted and subjective image throughout the entire process.

Maximising your chances

The economy, the labour market and politics are all facts of life. You have to deal with them on a daily basis, whether you like it or not, and there is little you can do to change this. Philosophising about it will not get you anywhere, except maybe a pat on the back for your brilliant analysis. Therefore, concentrate on what you actually *can* influence fully: yourself! Undertake every possible activity that will increase the chance of you getting that desired job. The good, old telephone can be a powerful tool, as you will read later in Chapter 4.

If you take jobhunting seriously, you have to see it as a *part-time job*. You will have to go hunting, and your prey is an employer. That is a better way to make a living than farming: waiting patiently for someone to call you again (sigh) to offer you that top position. Common mortals get calluses on their bottoms from sitting for so long. That is no option. Take the initiative day after day and be assertive in the journey that will lead to that sought-after job.

Look for a job intelligently and fanatically. That is the only way you can beat your competition. Do you work hard *every day,* or are you only fooling yourself?

Act like a professional athlete. Focus on your goals and be determined. Then you will be *mentally* busy with it 24 hours a day. When this stresses you, start observing relaxed animals for a while. Have you ever seen a worried cow in the meadow?

Dare to take a step back in your career path if it will help you to get working again. After all, you must pay your monthly bills.

As mentioned earlier in this chapter, time presents a well-known paradox for the unemployed: they have a lot of 'free time', but use it unproductively. A pity since you can achieve so much when you are 'temporarily' your own boss, learn so much, meet so many people, develop so many ideas, try so many new activities...

If you are serious about your job search, then we strongly advise you to spend four hours a day working on it: in the morning, afternoon or evening, whatever suits you best. In difficult times you will have to work hard to get the most out of the limited and decreased job market.

Personal progress report

To keep yourself on your toes, we recommend you report to yourself as a 'client' from the first day of your jobhunting project. We have set down the procedures for this in a separate chapter (Chapter 5).

Many people approach jobsearch intuitively. They come across a job vacancy, send an email, do not receive a response – and forget about it. This is no game plan. What you ought to do is to continually keep a detailed report of all your jobhunting activities. This will give you an overview of the process, at any given moment. The more you develop your contacts (with employers, with recruitment and selection agencies, within your network), the more difficult it will be to keep track of details and remember which person you have already spoken to, and about what.

It may help to keep a diary of your activities. Try to reflect on what you do by answering the following questions:

- Why have I done so much or so little work today?
- What have I done well or badly?
- What do I need to improve upon?

If it works for you, send yourself a daily email update.

'Regrettably you have not been chosen'

You often need a skin as thick as an elephant to deal with all the rejections. As a rule of thumb, the majority of jobhunters are rejected – a small consolation, of course. Just do the maths: if 100 candidates apply for a job, then 99 will not reach the end. It seems like a lottery; now it is time to get the winning ticket.

Most employers prefer emails to thank candidates for their application and reject them. That is quick and efficient – and as impersonal as a gunshot in the neck. In addition many recruiters find giving a verbal rejection to be difficult, just like any other bad news.

If you are dropped from the selection process, that does not mean you are rubbish. There will be enough new chances – every day! – if you stay alert and active. See the rejection as a small success. That may sound rather strange, especially after receiving the umpteenth rejection letter stating that 'Unfortunately, you have not been selected', since this results in anger, loss of self-esteem and self-respect, a feeling of inadequacy, bitterness and finally apathy. You need to prevent all that. Take charge! Get to work! Regard a rejection as a *learning experience*. Elevate your CV, covering letter and interview to an even higher level. After a dip you will continue more determined and active than ever before.

A rejection is a clear setback. Here is the bad news: there will be a lot more throughout your life, small and big. Prepare yourself mentally for them and take the punches. Until things go your way.

Summary

Main Points

1. A crisis also offers chances. Try to develop your insight into these opportunities.
2. It can be sensible (if you have the choice) to **not** change jobs.
3. If after many rejections you put looking for a job on the back burner, you only create new problems.
4. Set concrete and thus testable goals: how else will you know if you have met them?
5. Looking for a job requires action and hard work. Spend at least four hours a day jobhunting.

Worthwhile websites

Bestjobs.co.uk	Limited job bank
Monster.co.uk	Big digital job bank, with lots of jobhunting tips and extras
Ukkey.co.uk	Start page for 'everything', and that includes jobhunting
Wfs.org	Website of the World Future Society, where you can learn more about hot jobs and interesting labour markets and can stay abreast with future developments
Careerbuilder.co.uk	International job bank; easy to read
Governmentjobsdirect.co.uk	Working for the U.K. government, and much more

The next stop in the journey through the barren jobhunting landscape is *ego-research:* finding out who you are, what you can and what you want. That is the only way to put yourself on the map.

2

KNOWING:

WHO YOU ARE, WHAT YOU CAN DO AND WHAT YOU WANT

This chapter zooms in on the **K** from the KIRAP-CS process: knowing who you are, what your strengths and less strong characteristics are, what your competencies, talents and wishes are. Who you are and what you can do is reflected in your CV (curriculum vitae), your personal brochure, which will now be described in detail. You will make your own profile sketch, so that you can look for a job with a sharper focus. Your arrows need to be aimed at jobs that suit you. Self-knowledge and knowing what you can do and what you want will give you a better starting position in the job hunt. Unfortunately, there is only one expert in the world on who you are: you. So, take enough time to keep your 'expertise' up to date. If you want to beat your competitors – and they are almost always strong – then you will have to use all your weapons, including your CV. The quality of your CV is something *you* control, so work on it.

Starters or freshly graduated students and people re-entering the job market often experience more difficulty landing a job than seasoned jobhunters. This chapter deals with the specific problems that these groups will encounter.

Accept any job?

Even if you are willing to accept (within reason) any position in a difficult economy, you will nevertheless still be rejected numerous times. That can be due to your lack of specific motivation or potential for career growth. But in the case that you are chosen, the question remains whether or not you will be happy in your new job, whether you will 'stick around' and whether you have thrown your career overboard. (The long-term view.) In short, even if you think the situation is hopeless, it is wise to look for jobs that match your profile: who you are, what you can do and what you want.

Beware! Job-hopping may ruin your credibility in the eyes of employers. (Why should they invest in you, if you will just be hopping onto your next job? However, it *is* a strategy to accept a job under your level, 'park yourself', so you can climb out of the valley when the economy picks up.

Why do you need a CV?

A CV belongs to a jobhunter like Chelsea belongs to London. The best reason to make one (which should be reason enough!) is that employers demand it: no CV, no job. It is the way that recruiters and decision-makers can quickly make a selection out of the large number of similar men and women who apply, so that they can determine if the job requirements have been met. So the pile to the right (shortlist) makes it to the next round, the pile to the left does not and the one in the middle (the doubtful candidates) need to be re-examined.

A CV is *the* way to sell yourself. Make sure that your document looks better than your competitors' documents. A strong CV gets the attention it deserves. It inspires the reader because it contains what he or she is looking for in a new employee.

If you don't submit a CV, you can pretty well kiss these jobs goodbye. There are of course a number of exceptions:

1. You could choose to put together a resumé (less comprehensive than a CV). In it you describe your accomplishments, which could be connected to employers you have previously worked for. Some examples: 'After lengthy negotiations with external suppliers, the total purchase price was reduced by 15 percent.' 'Set up a new branch office in Manchester and managed it for the first two years.' 'Have closed down the IT department; ten employees

were made redundant and work was found for them elsewhere via an outplacement agency.' You can also describe your 'profile' in a number of sentences, including your special skills and strengths: 'I have ten years experience as a manager of a Tesco supermarket. My strength is people management. In addition I have a good background in finance and a reputation as an adept buyer.'

2. You are famous and/or 'everyone' knows you in your industry.

3. You are a performer (for example you play the piano) or have been awarded prizes for your professional skills (international recognition for your work as an advertising copywriter.)

4. You are related to or a long-time friend of the employer. He knows you through and through.

The CV is almost always accompanied by a covering letter (letter of application, letter of motivation). In Chapter 4 you will get tips about this.

Self-analysis: who am I, what can I do, what do I want?

Before you start looking for a job, you'd better have a good picture of who you are, what you can do and what you want. You need to develop a self-analysis or a personality profile, a portrait of yourself in words, so that you will not make the mistake of applying wildly for every vacancy you come across. Furthermore, it will help you get over the job interview threshold because you can back up your qualifications (with hard facts and examples).

Tunnel vision

Jobhunters often limit their search to vacancies that are directly related to their previous position, based on (perhaps 'misled by' is a better term) the question: 'What kind of work have I done before?' Via self-analysis you will be able to answer the question: 'What can I do?' The fact that you have done certain work in the past, does not mean you are doomed to stay within those confines for the rest of your life. Get out of that scary tunnel!

Do you take a chance applying for positions which happen to be outside your area of expertise or ambition? Or do you prefer to follow the expected pattern? Is it wise to make a change? Think of the risks. For instance, you may never be able to return to a job in your field of expertise or get your dream job, since professions change so quickly and you could get left in the cold. It becomes apparent during an economic downturn that employers are not very willing to take chances with regards to job applicants who want to make a career switch. Instead of 'experimenting' with less traditional candidates, employers will chose future employees who can be productive from day one. It is a tragedy that few people can change professions after having chosen the wrong study at a very young age.

Who am I?

The answer to this question will determine the direction of your job search. In general, people have a positive self-image: who doesn't think that he or she is socially skilled and acceptable or take initiative? Be strict but honest when you look at yourself.

Try not to be someone that you are not, because that will ruin you in the end. On the other hand, everyone can 'grow'. Are you an introvert? (Are you focused towards yourself rather towards others?) Do not force the situation by pretending to be the life and soul of the party if that is not who you are. Are you someone who likes to be the leader? Then you could probably be great in a coordinating position. You will probably not feel comfortable in a job where you have to do simple repetitive tasks. Are you very shy? Then a sales position where you have to make a lot of contact would be difficult for you. You would be better off in a position where shyness doesn't cause problems, or where you are allowed to be shy.

Some American career-planning books claim to know (via a code system) which personality types fit which types of jobs. If only it was that easy ...

TIP

Some people shoot themselves in the foot, ruin their chances again and again. For instance, they continually doubt everything, which makes life unnecessarily difficult for themselves and creates problems which others do not even see. They put the emphasis on the negative rather than the positive. Be your own best friend! Is that so difficult to do?

What can I do?

We will now concentrate on the skills, competencies and talents that can be developed through education or working. What are your strengths? Forget your weaknesses, because everyone has an abundance of these! Now the trick is to match your plus points with a job, so that you can positively *contribute* to what the employer is trying to achieve. How good are you at something and how have you shown that? Present compelling evidence!

If you actually possess these talents, you will need to sum up professional situations where you have acquired or applied them, or situations in your private life where they were put to use (less desirable). Do you have clear and convincing examples?

Even if you have little work experience (for example, because you have just graduated), you can still find relevant examples. The desired skills can be acquired just easily during an internship, a year chairing a club or participating in a student panel at your college or university (refer to 'Starters and People re-entering the labour market').

Specialist or generalist?

Do you pick a specialist or generalist position? Both have their pros (+) and cons(-):

Specialist	Generalist
Relatively little competition (+)	Can be put to work 'everywhere' (+)
Limited call for specialists (-)	A lot of competition (-)
Possibility to specialise further within a specialism (+)	Can be replaced by someone else or a machine (-)
Employer becomes dependent on you (+)	
Limited chance of being replaced by someone else or a machine (+)	

Transferable knowledge and skills

It makes sense to differentiate between skills that are related to a specific industry, organisation or location, and general skills that can be used almost everywhere. Look at the following examples of general skills. Supervising is a competency that can be used in any organisation. While there is a difference between supervising in a formal organisation and a creative one, the main points are the same. That also holds true for writing, no matter if it is writing letters, reports, manuals, handbooks, advertisements or any other kind of texts. If you have experience teaching children, it is a small step to teaching adults and you can probably apply these skills (after a certain amount of schooling) to training, coaching, sales or consulting. If you describe yourself as a researcher, you can investigate, test and experiment in many different ways and places.

Managing a production unit can be done just as well in a bicycle factory as in a bakery. If you can sell cars, you can also sell office supplies. (It is a matter of convincing people.)

Okay, there are distinct differences between these examples. But it is your job to persuade potential employers how much your previous jobs and the new job have **in common**. *Minimise the differences and emphasise the similarities!* The higher the level of 'abstraction' (using general rather than job-specific skills), the more similarities there are between jobs. And at the very highest level it all comes down to: paid work...

What do I want?

It is very important to know what kind of job you want (and what you want to achieve in life) – only then you can target your job search. You need to find out what your ambition and motivation is, but that is a difficult task for many. Some people do not figure this out in their lifetime... In addition, you may have to adjust your ambition during an economic downturn.

It is practical to have your 'dream' anchored in reality. And reality tells you that there are few jobs for museum directors or city planners, while there are many for account managers at banks. Sometimes you have to squash your dreams or lower your ambition.

In preparation for the job interview: if you have come to the conclusion that you want to be a manager or get into management, you should expect questions like: 'Why is that your ambition?', or 'What do you find so attractive about it?'

Where do I want to work?

In which industry or sector would you like to work? There are many different options, from art and culture to the fishing industry, from recreation to health care, from the food industry to fashion. Do you want to work in the service sector, wholesale, retail or industry? There is enough choice. Does it actually matter to you?

Most likely you know (in general) which industry you want to work in. But have you ever taken the trouble to compare them? Then this is the moment to do that. Go on a journey of discovery of the different sectors. You can start your search at your local Chamber of Commerce. If you only have (work) experience in one particular business sector, it will never hurt to broaden your horizons. Let your curiosity and inspiration take hold, via websites and professional/trade magazines. Are you eyeing high-tech jobs because you see a lot of potential in that sector, then keep the following points in mind:

- Include as much high-tech experience as possible in your present job or activity – and mention it on your CV.
- Maintain or work on your employer's website or web blog if possible. Or develop your own website or blog (or make one for a club you are a member of) and use it as a digital business card.
- Try to divide your responsibilities at your current job so that for instance 50 percent of your work has to do with high-tech.

There are two things you need to know about business sectors:

- Certain jobs are tied to certain industries. Due to your education, specialty or work experience, you may not be able to work in a different field. (Unless you make a U-turn of course.) A dentist can only choose to work with teeth and a pilot is doomed to work in the airline industry.
- There are functions where the sector is less important. If you are an *administrator* in the local tax office, in animal healthcare or in a publishing firm, the work remains generally the same.

Conditions of employment

What does a job have to have, as far as tasks, responsibilities, and so forth in order to meet your expectations? Based on your (work) experience up until now, you have most likely formed an idea of ideal work conditions. Whether or not a job is suitable depends not only on the combination of tasks, but also on a number of related factors, such as the commute (will you end up in a traffic jam?), work schedule (is there a schedule?), salary, training possibilities, working attire (formal or casual), kind of employment contract, career opportunities, your colleagues or whether there is a company restaurant.

Company culture

We have now reached the topic of ideology and all the formal and informal norms and values that are part of an organisation. What are the governing beliefs? What are the company's values? How and why are people judged?

At the same time you have your own values, the things that you find important and would like to see in your employer. Maybe it is honesty and an open culture, brotherhood and teamwork, social relevance and freedom (not a boss that is constantly looking over your shoulder). If it is the right choice, then your values and the organisation's match. If that is not the case, then sooner or later you will not feel at home there. So it is good to give this a second thought.

Unique Selling Points (USP's) for *this* position

After completing this self-analysis – you have more or less determined what your ideal jobs are. Let's make it concrete. How can you best qualify for this job in the eyes of the prospective employer, since they want to know: *what makes you suitable for this particular job?*

In order to answer this question as well as possible you have to throw your USP's into the ring. By doing so you can establish a clear advantage over your competitors, simply because they do not possess this unique combination of characteristics and experience. Maybe you have a number of 'double competencies', for instance a chemical engineering degree combined with sales experience, which naturally fit the relevant position. Or perhaps you have trade expertise and management experience – an outstanding combination. Put your tendency to be humble aside, if you have not already done that.

Creative abilities

Employers are always interested in creative spirits, because these are the people who achieve breakthroughs. These creative folks will not (cannot) be replaced by machines, or by cheaper workers in Asia. No-one can take away your creative abilities, but you will have to 'sell' them internally and externally. Are you creative at your job? What proof do you have of this?

Ambition and potential

How do you see yourself in the future? Not only are you thinking of this (or should be), but employers are also curious about it. It has to do with ambition – in other words, the desire to achieve something in the future – and with your potential: can you achieve more than what is being expected of you **now?** We call this your 'development potential'. Organisations have to think ahead. Do you fit into their plans further down the road? Do you want to, and can you, grow along with the company?

This is the way it is, but you can change the perception

You can hem and haw about the job responsibilities that you have never had or the schooling that you have never completed, while these may well be in the employers' job description. There is not much you can do to change this (within the confines of honesty). What is important is to open the eyes and ears of these future discussion partners to other important experiences and characteristics, which you are willing to 'lend out' despite your limitations. It comes down to 'selling' yourself.

From job to career development

What if you are completely in the dark about what you want to do? It is important to discover and define your talents. If you avoid doing this, then you run two risks:

- You will waste time and energy with jobs for which you are less suitable and to which you will be less committed.
- Later on in life you will become frustrated, because your true talents will be wasted, you never knew you had them, or you did not bother to take the risk to change jobs or careers.

On top of that, it is important that you find a job (career) which makes you happy, which you can deal with on a daily basis. (A bit of pressure at work is good. Too little will result in a permanent blank look in your eyes.) Or are you already envious of those stress-free senior citizens who do not know what a 'vacation' is because that is their daily reality?

For some people, building a career means taking giant steps. That is very attractive. But you can also make progress by taking a lot of smaller steps. Keep the long-term goal in sight as well as that (essential) 'next step'. Unfortunately, this can be difficult in times of economic malaise.

Career advice

Each of us chooses a unique life journey and career. Which choice have you made? Or do you let other people make the crucial decisions for you?

Some people have known what they want to become from a very early age. Others have their complete career mapped out – with or without the help of a career counsellor. Still others have not got a clue. Are you still in the dark? Make an appointment with a career counsellor. Don't expect miracles. And don't follow their advice blindly – that is *our* best advice. In the end it is *your* life.

> **TIP**
>
> Try to formulate your problem or question as clearly as possible before contacting a career counsellor. You will save not only time; the quality of the advice will be much better. A question like 'What do I have to do for the rest of my life?' will not get you any closer to a suitable job.

Career choice tests

Career choice tests are psychological tests which map out a person's career interests. They are based on the reasonable idea that if you want to be successful in a particular position, you should be interested in it. However, having a warm feeling about a profession does not imply that you will be a natural at it or that you possess the needed abilities, skills or competencies.

Some people like working with numbers (but not with language); other people like working with their hands (but not with 'people'). An analysis of the most important career tests shows that they cover a limited cluster of jobs of related professions. (Every job can be brought back to its roots or foundation, or a number of combinations of these.) The following categories are often found in these tests:

Technical	**Sciences**
Musical	Social (behavioural) Sciences
Commercial	Religious
Administration/figures	Sports
Literary/Writing	Care
Humanities and Social work	Medical
Pedagogical	Biological
Entrepreneurial	Management/supervisory
Creative/artistic	Persuasion/Sales

Perhaps making a career choice will be easier if you keep the above categories in mind, or a combination of them.

What does a profession mean in real terms?

If you do not quite know what kind of work particular future jobs or sectors will involve, then think about what your 'new' colleagues do on a daily basis. What does a **typical workday** look like? What are their tasks and responsibilities? What skills and knowledge do they need to carry out their profession? What education have they had and which one would they recommend? (And perhaps, how much do they earn?)

Which information do you need to come to a carefully considered assessment?

1. Some multinationals let their employees share their experiences on their website. They describe their daily routine, without any frills. You get to know what it is like in the trenches. (You will not find any serious criticism here, though.)

2. You can pose your questions to a news group or social network, such as Facebook, LinkedIn, MySpace, Twitter. The more your questions relate to the group, the more chance you have of getting a serious answer. You will find helpful members who will tell you about the pleasant and less pleasant parts of their jobs. Place a request and reap the answers! These kinds of networks work well for jobhunting as well (refer to Chapter 3).

3. There is a very detailed American free publication *Occupation Outlook Handbook* (www.bls.gov) which describes many professions and predicts the developments expected in these professions. Email friends and acquaintances, acquaintances of friends and friends of acquaintances who could possibly help you with your personal quest.

4. Pose your question on a forum, such as Monster.co.uk.

5. Maybe you are missing certain knowledge or skills. Look into the many (study) possibilities that are available in order to fill that (temporary) void.

Writing a CV

A CV (curriculum vitae) is a biography. More accurately formulated: it is a compact and chronological overview of your education, (work) experience and other relevant points. Your CV, the tangible end product of your knowledge and skills, will determine if you are invited for a job interview, your chance to 'score'. Is one standard CV enough or should you keep adjusting your biography during the jobhunting process? We will discuss that shortly (refer to 'Adjusting CVs: how far can you go?').

Ask yourself the following two questions when writing your CV:

- Will the reader get to know me with this CV with one glance (speed is essential!)?
- Does my 'CV image' fit the position?

!!!! DANGER !!!!

There is no generation that has ever had it so easy: send in your digital CV in a fraction of a second, here or to the other end of the world. The downside of this is the many mistakes to be found in CVs and application letters. Be aware of inaccuracies and sloppy work. Take care that everything is in mint condition, down to the last letter – literally.

Traditional, functional or dynamic CV

The traditional chronological (actually reverse chronological) CV is the most widely used CV. In this standard form it often begins with a listing of your schools and educational programmes. Then work experience is described. The idea behind this approach is to make one's (professional) life *transparent* and *verifiable*. While this kind of historical overview is easy to follow and the developments are evident, it demands accuracy from the writer. The disadvantage of this kind of CV is that it does not strike the reader, since it is so common.

In the functional CV the accent is more on skills and knowledge and less on development. This kind of document is often used by a person who has something to hide, for instance a certain gap period or unfinished schooling. It can also be chosen by those switching careers or when the emphasis is on the transferable skills.

The dynamic CV is a very abbreviated life story and makes reference to one's own homepage or blog (or other relevant websites.) It is modern, but requires the reader/visitor to take an active role in finding information. It is especially handy for ICT professionals or those who aspire to get into that industry.

For the purposes of this chapter we will concentrate on the traditional CV.

The traditional chronological CV

Here are the basic rules:

1. Describe your life with relevant titles (refer to the following example). The accent is on a chronological overview (years!) of your education and (work) experience. Note any degrees you may have.

2. Look at your CV as a brochure: you are selling yourself to employers, headhunters and others. Put your best foot forward. Pay attention to the choice of language: make it 'rich'. So not 'nice', but rather 'interesting' or 'ambitious'.

3. A CV must be absolutely infallable (you have picked up on the mistake... that should read *infallible* with an *i*). Mistakes reflect sloppiness, indifference, hastiness and disinterest, characteristics that will seldom help to have you invited out to the next round. Furthermore, your CV must be systematic

and consistent in its layout. That also says a great deal about you.

4. Imagine being a personnel manager who has to deal with all those application letters and CVs...Therefore, limit your CV to one or two sheets, if possible. Perhaps, you have produced a large number of publications or championship titles. Add these to your attachment.

5. Avoid 'holes' in your CV that indicate periods of time when you were not doing anything (worth mentioning). That is not done in our career-driven world, you should always be doing something productive. The personnel manager's worry is: where and how did you spend your time? On the beach? In a psychiatric asylum? On a long-term vacation behind bars? If your CV looks like Swiss cheese, how will you explain that in a job interview?

6. A CV should reflect your knowledge, skills, abilities and talents. Positions and names of (ex) employers are less important than duties, responsibilities and results. Emphasise your achievements in hard numbers, if possible. Note that these need to be 'significant' and meaningful. If necessary compare your achievements with those of others, for instance: 'wrote four cover stories per year (colleagues: two)'.

7. Name the promotions you received from an employer, the new titles that you had, for example: 'First junior consultant, then senior'. Don't to be too modest.

8. A clear and attractive lay-out makes the CV easy to read and shows your development. Have you alternated between study and work? Make that clear in your CV.

9. Keep it brief. Do not make it a narrative, but use a telegram style of writing. Keep in mind that while you spend days sweating over your CV to get it perfect, the busy personnel officer may take only one minute to make a selection. Your CV has to get their attention.

10. Nothing prevents you from giving your (digital) CV subtle background colour. You can distinguish yourself slightly from your competition. Be careful that the readability increases rather than decreases by these extra touches.

11. Less recent employment and schooling have less importance in your CV. The exact tasks in a starting function ten years ago are barely relevant. This also applies for school subjects and your thesis from six years ago.

12. If you use abbreviations in your CV (for schooling, titles, tasks, products, clubs etc), then you should assume that the reader is familiar with these. If not, write them out in full.

13. Make a note after each school period if you have earned the diploma (or certificate), the bachelor's, master's, PhD and so on. If you do not do this consistently, you will give the impression that you have unsuccessfully ended a course.

14. If you get stuck, get professional help. For instance, if you have awkward gaps in your career or you have writer's block. The adviser will consistently tailor your CV to the interview, which you will hopefully get with your CV. Keep in mind that it is after all your CV and not the adviser's. How you describe yourself must end up sounding authentic.

A traditional chronological CV could look like the following example. This model is quite extensive; in reality your CV could be much less detailed (no publications, patents, board memberships).

Curriculum vitae

Personal information

Name:	Andrew Walters
Address:	26 Cavendish Gardens
	London, SW14 8Q5
Telephone:	020-7385 6611
Fax:	020-7385 6612
Mobile phone:	07818 443 334
Marital status:	Married (one child)
Nationality:	British
Birth place and date:	Henley, 1 July 1970
Email:	awalters@hotmail.com
Weblog:	http://blog.walters.uk

Education

1999-2000	Post graduate diploma business studies, Erasmus University Rotterdam (diploma)
1987-1993	Business Economics, Brunel University (Master's)
1982-1987	GCE A levels, Montessori College London (diploma)

Trading, courses and development

2008	Financials for non-financials, MCB, Brussels (certificate)
2002	International negotiations, Grijzen Institute, Amsterdam (certificate)

Career history

2003 – present	**Media International Publishers, London**
Position:	International Sales and Marketing Director

Tasks/responsibilities:	Supervision of 10 employees; sale of British titles to foreign markets and purchase of foreign titles.
Results:	Yearly growth of business unit by an average of 20 percent.

1996-2003 **Endémolé, Staines**
Position: International Sales Manager
Tasks/responsibilities: Sales of programmes and syndications to foreign tv channels.
Results: Sold 10 percent or more over target each year

1994-1996 **PARA-TV, Oxford**
Position: Programme researcher for the news
Tasks/responsibilities: All the preparatory tasks for the financial and economic news items; selection of topics, interviewing candidates and jointly responsible for selecting visual material; involved in the purchase of foreign news items.

Additional work experience

2002 and 2007   Employed in Kenya as an English teacher via the Child Help International Foundation (during summer holidays)

Board functions

2007 – present   Chairperson of the residents' association for the Michaels' flat
2001 – 2005   Member of the Supervisory Council Forest View (psychiatric health care)
1999 – 2000   Secretary Rotary Club Staines
1992 – 1994   Board member Four Aces Tennis

Extracurricular activities

1995 – 1999	Editor _Soft Grass_
1986 – 1987	Chief editor school paper

Leisure activities

Tennis, wild water canoeing, writing film scripts, modern French literature, Japanese cooking, Rotary club member, volunteer in zoo (elephants).

Language skills

	Speaking	Writing	Reading
English:	mother tongue	mother tongue	mother tongue
Dutch:	Fair	None	Good
French:	Fluent	Good	Excellent
Japanese:	Fair	None	None

Publications

(Optional) in a chronological order.
(If it is a long list: in attachment.)

Licences (patents)

(Optional)

Awards

Best short story in the New Yorker (2005)
Honourable member of student fraternity Descartes (1992)
European junior rowing champion, skiff (1975)

Other relevant details

(Optional) Japanese mother

TIP

Make reference in your CV to your own website or blog, where interested employers can learn more about you. For instance, consider a list of completed projects or personal publications. Don't assume that your website will be flooded with visitors, but make sure that there is no damaging information to be found!

References

References do not belong on a CV. If you do want to make note of them, then limit it to 'Reference available on request' in the last sentence of your CV (refer to Chapter 5). The selection committee may want to know firsthand how you functioned at your current and/or former employer. Select your references with care! Ask them for their permission and 'work on' them if needed.

Internship on your CV?

If you have recently graduated, then it is appropriate to mention where you did your internship, which study you followed and any significant results. We know of a chemistry student who carried out independent research, on his own initiative, which led to a patent. If you graduated a while ago (more than five years), then an internship is irrelevant. Do not waste any time on this. It is outright pitiful to still be referring back to your internship experience after working for fifteen years – unless you are returning to that profession after having had jobs outside that field.

Omissions and anonymity on CVs

There may be situations where you want to omit certain pieces of information from your CV for private reasons or because you would be identified, for example:

- Place of birth or date, because you are afraid of (age) discrimination;
- Names of employers, because you work in a small sector and are afraid that your boss will be called;
- Leisure activity, because your hobby is not run of the mill: witchcraft and wicca.

Naturally, it is not a problem to omit certain hobbies from your CV. But if you omit other information, then you will actually be emphasising it ('He is probably old', 'She is probably not European', 'He must have left because of a dispute').

Once in a while the news media pay attention to the subject of anonymous job applications. The advantage is that a foreign name, with all the preconceived ideas about it, will not influence the selection process. It is a level playing field. That may be the case. But...

- In many job banks your name is already hidden from view. One less worry.
- An anonymous job seeker leads to suspicion, since it is an exception rather than the rule.
- If you use a pseudonym, think about the rest of the procedure when your real name will be revealed. How are you going to explain that?
- If you start changing information, like country of education, then you may have to change other pieces of information as well, and before you know it you will have a fake CV.

!!!! DANGER !!!!

Use your private email address in your CV. This address should look professional, so not something like partyanimal@aol.co.uk. Only use a business email address if you are certain that no-one else can read your mails from headhunters and nothing can 'leak' out.

Goals and personal profile

In American CVs there is often a career statement included – in other words a description of the kind of employment that you are seeking, for instance a position as *financial services director*. This should not be part of a CV, since it doesn't describe your career path. Put this information in letters to headhunters, employers or recruitment agencies when not applying for a specific position.

That also applies to the personal profile. For instance, we sometimes read in a CV that the person is dynamic and flexible, a team player and innovative and has a multicultural approach (whatever that might mean). We always come across very positive characteristics and never encounter: lazy, antisocial, aggressive, cannot get along with superiors, depressive, disloyal. Don't put these statements in your CV.

Attachments

You can add any number of (interesting) attachments to your CV. But is that wise? It is better to restrain yourself, since the recipient will feel more negatively towards you if they have to read them all. If you have accomplished so much, then it is better to take these documents to that long-awaited job interview and show them as proof.

If you still want to add attachments to your CV, then limit yourself to a list of your (most important) publications or a (summarised) list of completed projects.

Marks

Some employers are terribly curious. They will want to know your grade point average. (The interest in grades has diminished in the past few years.) Why this interest? First of all the recruiter can determine if you are as brilliant as you claim to be. A high potential ('hipo') with only low marks is contradictory. Secondly, it is a test of your honesty: your marks back up what you have said. And finally, your grades say something about your motivation. If you were inspired by a certain subject during your study and you want to qualify yourself further, then a relatively high grade would logically be expected. By the way, your terrible exam results before you finally got a passing grade will not be noted on your grade report.

What do you do if your marks are disappointing? You may want to say that you graduated very quickly, that is, faster than your classmates. Another situation is that your grades are not that relevant since you have chosen a different career path. Or because you were not interested in high marks. Why would you be – if you had volunteered to take part in all kinds of social activities, held (board)positions and/or had part-time jobs?

Add your grades as an attachment if it is specifically asked for or if the results are remarkably good. Otherwise: omit them!

Striking and original CVs

You can make a vocal recording (in audio or video) of your CV for the company's personnel manager where you are applying or you can freeze it into a block of ice. The CV will only have to be thawed out first. Before you take actions like these, ask yourself if the potential employer will value such an inventive and technical innovation. Mostly they will not, but in some sectors (advertising, marketing, IT, to name a few) it *may* go over well. It is also advisable to avoid bright (background) colours and special graphics. The fact that something is technically possible does not mean that it is valued.

Digital passport photo

Is it wise to include a photo of yourself on your CV? If you have a pretty face you may consider it. And for some (fashion or representative) positions it will be an advantage. But it may come across as vain or arrogant. If you choose to do this, then do it well! Photoshop your wrinkles away and touch up your skin tone. Maybe this will give you some pleasing results. But watch out! If the photo shows a vibrant thirty-year-old man and the recruiter thinks you look twenty years older, then the shock will be big and the chance of getting that job will be small.

Key words

Employers and recruiters are flooded with an endless stream of digital applications and CVs. They filter them (electronically) using key words, such as desired education and other requirements from the job advertisement.

This calls for special attention. Make a list of the key words from the job vacancy and be sure these are in your application letter and CV. For instance, if they are looking for an 'ambitious, recently graduated psychologist interested in research who speaks perfect German and French' (lots of luck, dear employer!), then these terms need to be found in your documents. If not, there is a big chance that you will end up in the wrong pile.

Adapting CVs: how far can you go?

It is handy to develop a universal basic CV. However, for certain job applications you may want to emphasise one or two points or omit others. In that case, adapt your CV. When you send out a lot of different CVs, it is a good idea to attach the CVs to the application letters (and to read them through before the job interview), so that what you say matches what you have written.

Once in a while an intermediary (headhunter, recruitment or selection agency) will ask you to adapt your CV for one of their clients. That mostly means padding one part (for instance your supervisory experience) and maybe omitting another. Do it!

How far can you stretch your CV? What can you legally omit or smooth over? Vacation jobs? Short jobs (less than four months)? What can you add to your CV life? A dental study that you have never taken? Remember: your CV is 'your business brochure' – so you need to balance between honesty and marketability.

An inspiring CV

You can choose to write your CV completely on your own or hand the task over to an expert and not put another gram of energy into it: 'Just make me a CV.' Completely turning it over is not an option; working together with an expert is. That is because you will have to be able to present your CV during the job interview. Then you need to know exactly what exactly been written – and you need to sound authentic.

'CV-evidence'

Is your CV foolproof? There is a big chance that you will get questions like these during the interview: 'You wrote that you improved the customer satisfaction by 10 percent in your organisation. How did you manage to do that? Where can you show me that in writing?' You will feel much more relaxed if you have the evidence with you. Make sure that document is in your portfolio! (Refer to Chapter 5.)

Questionnaires

As annoying as it can be, you will more than likely have to fill in a biographical questionnaire for each and every recruiter. Every time another form, but each time almost the same questions pop up. Sometimes it suffices to attach your own ready-to-send CV.

In some forms you will find less innocent questions like: 'What is your current salary? And what was your previous salary?' 'Do you rent or own your home?' What are your monthly housing costs?' 'Do you have any debts?' 'What is your management style?'

Starters and re-entrants

A true story – think about it:

> **Interviewer** *(with the job candidate's CV in front of him):* 'You do have a college degree?'

Candidate *(answers in a friendly way): 'Yes, that's right.'*
Interviewer*: 'Do you have a master's degree?'*
Candidate *(with a friendly tone): 'Yes, that's right.'*
Interviewer*: 'But do you have any competencies, what I mean is, what can you actually do?'*

Starters find it much more difficult to land a job when the economy is weak, since they cannot fall back on professional experiences that employers are looking for. If you keep getting knocked down, then you will never get the chance to get that experience! How do you find your way out of this stalemate? Don't be too humble! Even starters offer employers what they need:

1. The situation may not be as hopeless as everyone describes. If you are uniquely talented, then employers will find a place for you. But that is not the case for most people, far from it.

2. Starters are cheaper than those experienced workers. So convince employers to try a cheaper alternative and hire you.

3. It is often difficult for employers to make older employees redundant. A starter can be offered a half or one year contract, or an even shorter contract. That limits the boss's risk. Make them aware of this.

4. Explain that you have fresh ideas and up-to-date knowledge, along with the newest insights (from university). That can be expected of you.

5. You are easy to train and flexible, not stuck in a rut. You are able (and willing) to work long hours due to your youthful age and enthusiasm.

6. You have interesting contacts (for instance from your internships).

TIP

Are you a 'hipo'? Take the initiative and do not wait for vacancies to appear, but actively make contact with prospective employers. High potentials are *always* welcome – even when there are no immediate job openings. The reason: talent is constantly being hunted.

'I have nothing to report!'

Young graduates, with little life experience and a paper thin CV: how will the labour market react to them? It is every applicant's fear to have nothing to report. Our experience at Psycom has shown that everyone has gained many experiences in their lives, with stories to tell, of which a number belong in a CV. We hope to awaken your creativity with the following examples: you have surely done something outside your studies (during your time at college), possibly gone on a study tour or organised a ski holiday for classmates, regularly contributed to a faculty bulletin, organised a gala-evening, set up a sport tournament, served on a commission or were bass player (or maybe leader) in a band.

And what can a re-entrant report?

- Coordinated household logistics (time management!);
- Performed as amateur actress for many years (perseverance);
- Directed a play two times (leadership);
- Successful completion of modular study at the Open University (concentration);
- Built own home (technical insight);
- Secretary for a residence association (coordinating);
- Planned and organised yearly family reunion four times (organisational talent);
- Studied Spanish here and in Spain (quick learner);
- Taught elderly people to use the internet, email and Skype (teaching).

There is no need to be worried if you cannot make use of the above ammunition. Ask yourself: what special talent can I offer?

The younger you are, the less experience you will have. So your CV is super-skimpy. That's why some starters have the tendency to 'fatten up' their CVs. They knock something together that looks good and they even begin to believe it themselves. The problem is that in a (heavy) selection process all this padding will be pulled apart. Will the CV survive this? If the interviewer uncovers only one big exaggeration or fib, then he will go looking for a second one and then it is game over.

It is thus important to stay close to the truth. However you can make the facts look more attractive – you still have to sell yourself! If you have a temporary job that does not match your education level and/or career goal, you could expect an interview question like, 'What do you do for work?' Do you want a better answer than what is on the tip of your tongue, then approach it creatively. Imagine you have a sales position in a shoe shop. A logical and easy answer would be: 'I am a (shoe) salesperson', or: 'I sell shoes at...' A more convincing reaction is: 'I advise and help clients with their choice of...' Do you work at a telephone helpdesk, then a better explanation, with more allure, is: 'I diagnose and solve clients' problems.'

During your school years you may have taken part in extracurricular activities. Were there courses like photography or script writing? Which extra things did you do and why? Can you take advantage of these skills in the targeted position? These activities, that are not connected with your study major or future profession, prove that you are willing to go that extra mile.

If you have little work experience, take examples from all your school experiences, internships, vacations and clubs: anything that you can think of. List all the activities that you have done with success and pleasure in your life, write down the sub-skills that were needed and translate these into specific accomplishments that accounted for your success. To convince you that there are always – no matter how limited your official work experience is – relevant facts worth mentioning which reflect your skills, read the example of the paperboy who works his way up to the top.

Work experience

At school

- Designed and distributed posters for talent night. Consequently asked to administer publicity material. Received many complements for work.
- Responsible for about half of the theatre set for the annual school play. After the second year I was entirely responsible for the task.
- Coordinated assignments for the other volunteers.

Free time and holidays

- Did repair work for the elderly in the neighbourhood. Unplugged sinks, installed water heaters, fixed electrical problems. I got a lot of jobs via word of mouth.

A handy trick for yourself is to keep defining every activity in terms of knowledge, skills and attitude, or what you have learned from it. For example: 'that means that I can delegate very well.' Translate this during the interview, when the interviewer does not make the connection himself.

Summary

Main points

1. During difficult times it is wise to 'park yourself' in a job.
2. It is necessary to compose a CV. It may be necessary to have different CVs for the different categories of jobs you apply for.
3. Beware of tunnel vision, in which you limit your job hunt too 'close to home'. Think in terms of transferable skills and knowledge. Convince employers that your last (present) job is comparable with the future one.
4. After self-analysis you will be better able to decide which jobs suit you and which Unique Selling Points you possess.
5. Starters have more work experience than they assume to have. Dare to be creative!

Worthwhile websites

Monster.co.uk	Examples of CVs
Resume-resource.com	Examples of CVs
Workthing.com	Career tools
Prospects.ac.uk	For graduate careers
Mbaplaza.eu	Overview of European MBA programmes
Coursesplus.co.uk	Catalogue of training courses

After searching for yourself it is now time to look for the (right) jobs. That is what we will deal with in the next chapter.

3

INVESTIGATE:

WHERE ARE THOSE JOBS?

Now we have reached the I-phase of jobhunting: carrying out the investigation. The easiest way to do this is to find an attractive job at home in front of the computer through an internet job site. Just mail that CV, get invited to that job interview and *voila*, the job is yours. Regrettably, it does not work that way during difficult times. You will have to do more. Where are you going to find those jobs? We will describe a number of possibilities. And in the final chapter we will cover a few more, in case you have not succeeded in landing a job.

When you locate what seem to be attractive job vacancies, you have first to carefully analyze them. If it is not possible to pass a judgement, start looking on the internet and talk to people in that profession, until you can accurately assess the vacancies. The next steps, calling, emailing and writing, will be covered in Chapter 4.

You and the economic tide

We are all dependent on the ups and downs of the economy: one moment there is an abundance of great jobs, the next moment the supply has shrunk. Whatever the economic situation, you will *have to* track down published job vacancies. If you come across too few (in your sector or area of interest), then there are a number of things you will *want* to do to increase the number of possible openings. You have to be *pro-active*; get those hands out of your pockets, and be less choosy about what you would like (as far as salary, commuting, or a challenging job is concerned).

Job Titles

Nothing is more misleading than job titles. In the past someone was a cleaner, nowadays an interior cleaning specialist. The salesperson from a few years ago is now an account manager. And the team leader has moved up to unit manager. What's in a name? You are probably well aware of the most common job titles in your work area, but there will also be many positions which you have never heard of. This makes jobhunting on the basis of job title difficult. Therefore, look at job *descriptions* as well.

Mission impossible

So you find a job which matches your knowledge and skills perfectly. Or not? Most likely there are a number of holes in your job profile. There are always employers who are looking for that super employee who can do everything (and does not cost anything either!), and the advertisement reflects their 'ideal candidate'. It could just be your dream job. Depending on the job market, both parties will adjust their demands, for practical purposes. The difficult question that you have to answer is: do I fulfil (almost) all of the requirements stated in the ad? And if not, what can I do about that?

If you are applying for a traineeship at a multinational, the job title implies that you will be in training and that certain knowledge and skills are missing. That does not mean that you will start off with a blank slate. In order to succeed at the job you will already have acquired some knowledge and skills. Exactly which ones may be difficult to pin point. You will not learn much from the job advertisements since employers are always looking for that perfect employee. You can take action based on whether the position requirements are realistic:

1. On a regular basis read magazines with information about the labour market and switching careers. You will find interviews of people working in different positions and employers who discuss their hiring policy. On the internet you will come across a large number of sites with a lot of (often superficial)

information about positions, companies and developments in the job market.

2. Find out who can inform you about the daily responsibilities of the position you have your eyes on.

Job vacancy analysis

There is much that you need to know about a position – and not all of it (and sometimes very little) can be found in the job vacancy ad. **Decoding** ('deconstructing') it is a profession in itself.

The employer is looking for the ideal candidate and puts an advertisement in the newspaper, on internet, wherever. How is a job ad made? Sometimes, it is written, following a certain procedure, by a team, with the help of an external advertising agency, which spends long hours perfecting it. However, the following scenario is also possible:

> **Head of Personnel**: *'We need to place a job vacancy for a product manager right away.'*
> **Assistant**: *'We still have that advertisement from four years ago. Shall I find it?'*

Sometimes there is hardly a thought put into the qualifications a candidate needs to have. They are looking for someone to fill a position that has always required a certain college graduate. So the ad asks for these college graduates while there are a large number of suitable people available without this diploma. In other words, the person writing the advertisement may not be up to date (anymore) with the developments in the labour market. But if every department contributes their two cents worth, it will result in a flavourless, colourless and bland compromise, or a hollow and 'political' job vacancy text.

Another problem is when the text and the graphics of some personnel advertisements look absolutely fantastic, but the truth is far removed from this perception.

Three tasks = 80 percent

Can you imagine the (average) workday in the sought-after position? What does he or she do during the day? What are the important tasks and responsibilities and how much percent of the time is spent doing each of them? Which demands from this vacancy are *essential* and which are less believable? In general, you can assume that the three most important tasks of all functions account for 80 percent of the workday. Call up the contact person from the job ad, if necessary, and ask what they mean by...? Which tasks does the person have to do? How much time is taken up by...?

Does the vacancy suit you?

If it turns out that you miss too much essential knowledge or too many skills to hold down the desired position, then you will have to find out if you can fill these gaps, and if so, how much effort and expense it will cost. These are your best options:

- Begin at a lower position that will be a starting point, from which you get the chance to grow into the desired job.
- Begin with a position where you can gain valuable experience and at the same time take specific training and courses to reach your desired level.

Does the job vacancy fit with who you are? You are the one who will have to explain – *convincingly* – why the combination of you and the job is like a marriage made in heaven. (And which flaws will you have to cover up?) Be aware of the many facets of a position that can make use of your characteristics and strong points. To name just a few:

- *eye for detail*
- *artistic trait*
- *independent worker*
- *technical insight*
- *verbal communication skills*
- *organisational skills*
- *commercial insight*
- *flexibility and adaptability*
- *ability to concentrate*
- *meticulousness*

- *accuracy*
- *charisma*
- *patience*

- *mathematical skills*
- *leadership*

Checklist

Answer the following questions:

- Is the job title clear? Do you know what an 'egghead' is and does? And a 'BU-manager'?

- Is it obvious what the job description means? Or is it just well-written abracadabra?

- Are the job responsibilities in *order of importance*, according to the employer. If that is not clear, then make an evaluation of the ranking yourself.

- Which key words jump out at you? What do these *mean* to you? And what do you miss in the text?

- Describe which experience and schooling you have related to each aspect of the job.

- If you don't have the required experience, look for parallels. (For example, they are asking for something that most often is called .... by other companies. See also 'Transferable knowledge and skills' in Chapter 2.) Which knowledge and skills are in your opinion necessary for the combination of tasks you want, how many of these are you missing?

- Are you able to quickly acquire the missing knowledge or skills? If so, how?

Personnel advertisements often only describe the top of the iceberg of what a job entails. Most likely, you will always have too little information and it will be assumed that you know a lot (implicit knowledge) about the position. You will not encounter the following detailed job description in an advertisement, but you will need to have or get this knowledge.

Example: account executive (AE) advertising agency

First of all, a difference must be made between big and small advertising agencies: at a small firm, the AE is a jack of all trades, someone who can help his clients in all different areas (for instance writing copy for ads and brochures). We will describe the more specialised AE position at a larger agency. Take note of the words in italics.

- The A E represents the agency at the client's and the other way around. He is wearing two hats, *looking after* the interests of two parties.

- The agency has three in house disciplines: creativity (art direction and copy writing), account direction (client contact, AE position) and marketing/account planning/media planning. The AE must be able to *work together*, to *teamwork*.

- The AE must give his colleagues a clear *summary*, which mirrors the client's wishes and views. They will develop their part of the advertising campaign.

- The final plans must be approved by the paying customer. That means that the AE (alone or with his colleagues' assistance) is able to *present* and *convince*.

- The AE must be a *coordinator* and a *source of information* for the client: how and where do we set up the next dealer meeting? Should we or should we not advertise in this new magazine? When and how should we do our pr for this new product? And our advertising?

- The AE's *know-how* must include the following disciplines:
  - advertising (theory, effectiveness, research, mass communication);
  - graphics (materials, standards, possibilities, prices, etc);
  - marketing;
  - marketing research;
  - consumer behaviour (end user and professional buyer);
  - design (packaging);
  - direct response;
  - telemarketing;
  - printed media (working, planning, purchase);
  - e-media;
  - public relations.

  (Of secondary importance are topics such as sales techniques, distribution, organisational studies and management.)

- The AE must *sell* for his employer. After all, his agency needs to invoice billable hours.

- Related to sales are the purchasing tasks. Think about negotiating good deals from suppliers for his clients.

- It should be clear that there is an element of *trust* involved:
  - The AE acts a *sounding board*, a communication partner, a willing listener for the client.
  - The AE picks up a lot of information about the goings on inside the client's organisation, its turnover and profitability, new developments and products etc. *Ethics* (confidentiality) play an important role here.

Climbing over hurdles

There are three hurdles or problems that will hold you back from reaching your goal or getting the desired job. The first one you cannot do anything about: there is no match at all. You just happen to not be an astrophysicist with ten years of national and foreign work experience. And you do not have the ambition to become one either, so we might as well forget about that one.

The second hurdle is that once in a while you just do not fulfil **one or more** of the requirements. But maybe you will succeed, with a bit of pushing and pulling, to convince the employer or intermediary. You have to use every trick in the book!

The third hurdle you can easily step over, only you are the one holding yourself back. These are the kinds of problems that you *alone* must overcome:

- You wander aimlessly through jobhunting land. Where should you look? You do not have a clue. (While in the next phase you must convince an employer that you are, without a doubt, the right person for the job.)
- You have no time or you are too busy. (So, looking for a job is not a priority for you. You can easily solve this problem.)
- You miss that creative spark to sell yourself in writing or in an interview. (Get help of a professional or a friend.)
- The jobs which you are applying for offer a lower salary than desired. You are not sure yet, that you want to or have to take a step back.
- With one short course and that certificate you are 'in business'. But you cannot make that first step. (Do so!)

It is easy to 'lock' yourself up with a computer to look for jobs and wait to see if there is anything that suits you from the wide range of choices. But that can result in an unsatisfactory return on your efforts, in other words: no job. Get out of your shell and approach organisations.

Where do you find job vacancies?

The more difficult times are, the more channels you will have to investigate to find suitable vacancies. Make use of all forms of media so that you won't miss one single potentially fitting published or unpublished job opening. Many roads lead to Rome, and in this case to a job. We will discuss a number of sources, including the less accessible ones, leading to 'hidden' job market.

TIP

You want to look for jobs during economic downturns in sectors which are more or less recession-proof. Think of the food industry. People need to eat every day, don't they? Don't forget (national, county and municipal) governments, healthcare, defence, education and charitable foundations – in short, go through all the non-profit sectors.

We will discuss the following sources of job vacancies:

1. Job sites and megabanks (internet)
2. Company sites
3. Printed media (newspapers and trade journals)
4. Recruitment and selection agencies and headhunters
5. Networking
6. Temp and interim agencies
7. Jobcentre Plus
8. Open job applications
9. Radio and tv commercials
10. Internships
11. Job fairs
12. Advertising yourself
13. Other 'jobs' and contracts

1. Job sites and megabanks (internet)
(easy to find jobs?)
The internet has developed into *the* watering hole for job predators. The job sites are by far the favourite sites. But the electronic highway also offers other possibilities; of these we will discuss a few.

We would like to make a distinction between general and specific job sites. You will have to determine yourself, by trial and error, which are the best relating to your job, level and other search criteria. The more often you are on internet, the smaller the chance is that you will miss out on a vacancy. Develop a big fishing net made up of job sites and mega job sites. The latter are collections of vacancies published on other sites, the so-called second-hand market.

The digital supply of jobs seems considerably bigger than it really is. Many are duplicated, because the employer and the intermediary place their vacancies on more than one website. Furthermore, these are also selected by all kinds of search machines and mega job sites. You may come across three times as many 'vacancies' than actually exist.

If you do not find openings in your field on all the job sites, on company sites, on websites of executive searchers or through other digital channels, that does not mean that there are none to be found. The only conclusion is that they are not made available via these websites and can only be obtained via recruitment and selection agencies or via trade journals. (Sometimes a login code is required for trade magazines, which is only available to their subscribers.) Do not be lazy or lose your focus. Pick up the telephone and get on the road, for example for a 'network talk' (we will deal with this in point 5).

!!!! DANGER !!!!

Once in a while we encounter the worst kind of suspicious job vacancies, similar to a Golden Pyramid. Beware shadowy offers, especially if you have to invest money in a job or a product.

If you want to limit your search results on internet, then add 'and' to the query ('sales manager' and 'Midlands'). Do you want to enlarge your search? Then add 'or' to your query ('desk researcher or analyst'). It is also possible to make use of a 'wildcard': if you type in 'traffic', then all the positions to do with 'traffic' will pop up on your screen, like traffic expert, traffic engineer, traffic tower manager and traffic regulator.

It can be useful to make a schedule for your vacancy search, as shown in the example below. You have been warned: it is very time-consuming!

Monday	Tuesday	Wednesday
Monster.co.uk	Careerbuilder.co.uk	Headhuntersdirectory. com
Stepstone.com	Direct.gov.uk	Jobs.ac.uk
Allthejobs.co.uk	Prospects.ac.uk	Academicjobseu.com
Careers.ed.ac.uk	Bestjobs.co.uk	Mercuriurval.com
Trade journals	Trade journals	Trade journals

Thursday	Friday	Saturday
Ukjobsguide.co.uk	Jobs.guardian.co.uk	Weekend newspapers
Unmahjobs.com	Australiarecruit.net	Relevant 'specials'
Jobrapido.co.uk	Timeshighereducation. co.uk	Governmentjobsdirect. Co.uk
Trade journals	Trade journals	

On automatic pilot

Job sites have a convenient and time saving device: the *update service* (also known as robot or job agent) which automatically keeps you up to date – if you want to be, of course – on the latest jobs in their file. So you don't need to be a slave to your computer and continually check their sites. While you are sleeping, your job is sent to your home. It cannot get any easier than that.

Another possibility: deposit your CV in the CV-banks of your favourite job sites (via a standard form) and describe yourself with a catchy advertising slogan, without having to continually plough through the available jobs. After you have registered, let the recruiters do their work. If you want to increase your chance of being 'caught' – and that is what you want – do the following:

- Advertise yourself by using a distinctive and intriguing headline ('ad slogan') above your CV.
- Put in the keywords that 'your' employers and intermediaries are looking for and 'fall for'.
- Recruiters are always interested in the newest CVs. You can easily arrange to stay 'fresh' and on top of the digital pile by making small changes in your on-line CV one or two times per month, for instance by changing the slogan or a few words of text.

TIP

If you submit a general CV, you will probably get a lot of reactions, but of the right nature? Is your CV very specific, than you may have to wait a long time to get a response. Try to find a suitable compromise.

Social networks

More and more people have a personal page on MySpace, Facebook, LinkedIn or similar smaller sites, where they post information about themselves and photos. You can make good use of this in your daily job search. Let the world know that you are looking for a job, and be specific about what you want. (A weblog will not be effective for this purpose, since you are only known in a small circle of people.)

LinkedIn is a worldwide network for professionals. Considering that headhunters are also part of this 'community', and could read your profile, you may indicate that you are looking for this or that position. Is that an effective approach? This question is just as difficult to answer as what the hit rate of the CV banks is. But what do you have to lose? The first step is to register yourself by LinkedIn.com – it will not cost you anything, except time. Pay attention that your page reflects the image you have in mind. Make it as easy as possible for the hasty headhunters, by indicating in a *summary* what kind of jobs you are looking for and what your strengths are. You also have the possibility to ask other LinkedInners to write a recommendation for you. There may be some good sales arguments among them. Furthermore, you can join specific groups or make a group yourself. On this social website you can also find out if there are employees, who work at the firm that you are interest in. These contacts will give you valuable insights into the company. You also have the possibility to send these employees 'private' mail.

You can also 'twitter' jobs, in other words make use of Twitter.com to inform your twitter friends quickly, concisely (maximal 140 letters, to be precise) and frequently that you are 'in the market' for a (new) job. Twitter's goal is to keep your friends constantly up to date about your life, so why not use it. Starting one of these micro-blogs is very fast and easy.

Facebook and MySpace are not that businesslike: they are meant for friends (and that is a rather loosely defined term in social networks) to keep each other up to date of goings on in their private lives. Try to be introduced to someone in this secondary network via this social network.

Modify your weblogs and personal pages regularly: every time you add something, others will know that you are 'digitally alive'. Some people get addicted to these social networks. Do not let that happen to you.

There are also possibilities via chatrooms, according to theory...

Check your presentation on the internet regularly. Employers may – probably *will* – 'google' you to find all kinds of information about you. (There are different possibilities to protect private information.) What will they find? Your name on the website of the local drama club, where your Hamlet performance is praised? (Not bad.) A little film that you put on Youtube to let the whole world enjoy your sexual shenanigans. (Not good.) Most things on internet are very innocent and not serious, but make sure that you do not complain about your boss or work (or both) or disclose that you really have not graduated.

2. Company sites
(button with or without vacancies)

Most companies publish their job openings on their own website. (Cheap!) Visit your favourite employers on a regular basis. One problem is that many employers do not want to let on that there are no vacancies (and thus are not doing well). All the filled vacancies are removed incredibly slow and even nonexistent jobs are added under the vacancy button.

TIP

If you want to find these jobs more quickly: search via Google with the particular company name and 'vacancy'.

!!!! DANGER !!!!

It is not always evident when a job page has been updated. Some state that they were updated 'today', while it is only the date that has changed, automatically. It can turn out that a vacancy was filled years ago!

3. Printed media (newspapers and trade journals)
(the tradition continues)
In the past (not even that long ago) newspapers were the way to spot jobs. There are still a lot of positions published in the national, regional, daily and weekly and neighbourhood papers, but internet has surpassed the newspapers' top position.

Do you know which trade journals could be useful for you since they publish personnel advertisements? Be aware that not all trade journals publish vacancies on their website! Reading a trade journal can be handy when you want to orientate yourself in a new profession.

4. Recruitment and selection agencies and headhunters
(hidden jobs)
More and more jobs are being 'handed out' via middlepersons. So it is smart to have contact with them as well. These agencies work for you for free; only the unscrupulous outfits will charge you. The employer that ultimately hires you pays for the agency's services.

Register yourself and find out what they can do for you, whether or not in the long term. Inform them about the type of jobs you are interested in and/or qualified for.

Executive recruiters

All European countries are blessed with many executive recruiters, also-called (but not entirely correctly) headhunters. Their number is bobbing up and down with the economic waves. It is an unlicensed profession, so anyone can practice it. Executive searchers are the more expensive siblings of the recruitment and selection agencies and recruit for higher positions.

Mostly they find you, as the name suggests. But you can also take the initiative and look into the hidden labour market that they represent. (Do it!) Waiting until you are called up is a risky strategy when not one single recruiter knows who you are.

Select ahead of time which intermediary you want to work with. Consult for instance headhuntersdirectory.com.

Headhunters, the estate agents of hope, can do even more for you:

- They help you to make a big jump in your career.
- They present jobs which you may not have thought of yourself.
- They inform you of your market value.
- They negotiate on behalf of you with the potential employer about salary and the other benefits. (This is not out of sheer love for you, but to make sure the deal with his client goes through.)
- They keep you informed about possible future vacancies.

Do *not* get in touch with headhunters for a friendly chat about your career or to ask advice about the career path you should take. They have no time for that. Get in touch with a different specialist for those kind of questions.

Registering and first contact

A systematic approach goes like this:

1. First make a selection of agencies that could do something for you. Assess for instance for which sectors and functions

(level) they work for and the salary level which they negotiate for.

2. Call the chosen agencies; explain who you are and what you want. Ask them if they have or will have suitable positions for you in their portfolio. Make a list of discussion topics and key words ahead of time, so that you won't forget any essential points.

3. Offer to submit your CV. If you get a positive reaction, then send it off as quickly as possible – unless you come to the conclusion that you need to adapt your CV. Also include a covering letter in which you refer to the pleasant conversation that you (just) had with Ms X. To strengthen your attack you may consider submitting extra documents. Think about an article about you or a photo of you with the president of the company where you work(ed) etc.

4. Call several days later and ask if your CV has been received in good order, and your foot is in the door.

5. Hopefully you will get an invitation for an interview for a specific job or just to exchange information. But if this does not happen...

6. ...Maintain regular contact with this person. (Plan a contact moment once every four weeks.)

It will take at least two months before you get a job via a recruitment agency or headhunter. When a recruiter is finished with his preparatory work for the client, then different candidates will be introduced to his principal, followed (hopefully!) by an assessment and contract negotiations.

If *you* are approached by an agency or headhunter you ask for time to think it over and you request additional information: regarding the job description and the job's responsibilities, the salary and other benefits.

When you invite yourself for an audition – in fact a 'sales pitch' – you will have to show what you are made of, with strong arguments and excellent presentation skills. Since you will make use of an intermediary it is important to not be too specific during the talk.

Try to not place the emphasis on the type of positions you would like to have. The bigger your repertoire of skills is, the more choices you will have.

The vague promise of 'we will keep you on file' (or 'in our portfolio') sounds great, but is mostly the kiss of death. It is just a nice way of saying good-bye and farewell.

TIP

Make reference to your personal website for more information only if that will add to your strengths.

---

5. Networking
(get more out of your (new) acquaintances)

Where people used to talk about exploiting 'the old boys network' or 'relationships', nowadays this is called 'networking' – and it works. Shy people absolutely hate it. They do not want to 'bother' others, ask for favours or stick out in a crowd. They easily forget that they are also making a contribution to a network: it is a two-way street. The fact that you pluck up the courage and look for a job gives many employers a positive impression.

A company's employees and business relations are often a good source for potential new hires. How do you get in on this? Through your network! Sometimes a job still has to be created at the moment that you are invited for a meeting.

Do not expect that every networking discussion will immediately lead to a job. But assume that you will hear something, a tip, a lead that could bring you closer to that desired job. Do not wave your CV around, but make it clear that you are in the market for a job. Make sure that your CV is close at hand, in case it is asked for. Or promise to send off a copy today. Your discussion partner can immediately forward it to his contact.

Thanks to a networking contact, who puts himself out for you, you are not an unknown face when you appear for an interview. And if your 'networking discussion partner' cannot help you further, then it is not the end of the story: ask him or her who *can*. Due to the fact that you make a lot of contacts (= shooting), sooner or later you will come across useful contacts (= hitting).

TIP

Try to find a sponsor, someone who believes unfailingly in you and can open doors for you that would otherwise be kept shut.

Neglected networks

How often have you come across people that do an excellent job every day and arrive home with a tired and satisfied feeling? And we should also add that they completely neglect their (professional) network. They only realise that when they end up on the cobblestones, and then it is too late. Do not let that happen to you. Take good care of your network, *now*.

Another problem that occurs is when a change of career (lawyer become HR-manager) does not turn out as expected and one considers returning to one's original profession. But unfortunately, the old network does not exist anymore...

Which relationships do you make use of?

A network can be informal, made up of friends and acquaintances. It can also be formal, think about professional associations, societies or user platforms. If you are or can become a member of a sports club or a service club like Rotary, Roundtable or, Junior Chamber (JCI) then you will notice the good networking possibilities. Study groups and political parties can also fulfil an important role. The same applies of course to industry associations, user groups (of a particular hardware or software), associations, unions, etc. Get as much as possible out of your membership! Attend meetings – even if it bores you and you cannot see the usefulness of it. Still better: volunteer for a commission or as a board member. You will get to know more people – and get to know them better.

Do not forget to put in your network: people in key positions in their organisation (such as marketing, advertising and personnel managers), neighbours, old colleagues, teachers, college friends and classmates, lawyers/solicitors, management consultants, clergy, journalists (of trade journals) and interim managers.

TIP

Make a selection from your contact list of the people who intersect different social networks. Through them you will get valuable new contacts.

You can quickly do business with people who you know personally, your primary network. Other relationships may 'hear' a lot. If they are well established in a certain sector, they could mean a lot for you. The secondary network is made up of relationships of relationships, people that you do not know but who are interested in getting in touch with you.

If someone in your network has arranged a meeting for you, let him or her know afterwards (an email does not cost anything) where it has led to. A thank-you note and feedback is always appreciated.

At first glance it sounds great if you have a few Big Bosses and HR-managers in your network. However, these are seldom the decision-makers for your potential job. (And no-one would like to be accused of nepotism.) So make sure the top dog refers you to a department head.

Goal oriented networking

Networking is work and so it costs time and energy. Therefore, you must have concrete *goals* in mind:

- Receptions and cocktail parties (however tiresome they can be) are good opportunities to meet new people. Have the courage to mingle with the guests. Don't be shy. Give out your business card left and right. (And maybe you will meet a headhunter!) Forget about safely chatting with friends and acquaintances, but mingle. Think of a suitable opening line before you strike up a conversation with a perfect stranger.
- It goes without saying that conventions and symposia offer interesting programmes, but they are also outstanding meeting places. Make it your goal to talk to the top three speakers and get their business cards. Even better, organise your own reception party or network meeting.
- Your friend's sister is a personnel manager in the sector you want to work in. Call her up! You want to know which companies may have vacancies now or in the new future and which corporate culture would suit you the best.
- No doubt a bond will develop between participants at longer educational courses. 'Fresh' information will be shared between them, including upcoming and/or existing job openings.
- An internet forum or a social website like LinkedIn can be useful, but do not pin all your hopes on these.
- For starters, it is wise to get in contact with former colleagues and alumni.

Chance meetings

We know someone who found an attractive position through his dog. Not that the canine could talk, but the pet owner would start a conversation with anyone who was also walking their dog. That is how he got to know a woman who confided that her husband was looking a project manager, while the dog owner had already applied for that kind of job at many companies. Coincidence? Yes. But without that conversation, these two parties would have never met. The bad news is that buying a dog doesn't automatically lead to a job offer...

6. Temp and interim agencies
(the temporary solution)

More and more jobs are 'flexible'. Professionals no longer are embarrassed about being a temp or interim staff. The temp agency is an intermediary between businesses that are looking for (temporary) employees and jobhunters. Let them know what kind of job you are looking for and what your experience is. The temp agency will get to work for you (or not). Often the temp job will become a permanent position, because the employer has gotten to know you (rather risk free) and like what they see.

There are both general and specialised agencies, for instance ones for medical personnel or older people, paralegals, etc.

TIP

For some job seekers an interim placement is a sensible option, until the economy picks up.

7. Jobcentre Plus
(the biggest job bank)

We are talking about the government employment service which has the biggest job bank in the country.

Launched in April 2002, Jobcentre Plus brought together the Employment Service and parts of the Benefits Agency that delivered services to working age people. Its aim is to help more people into work and more employers fill their vacancies, and to provide people of working age with the help and support to which they are entitled.

In addition to an enormous online database of jobs (www.direct.gov.uk/en/Employment/Jobseekers) there are a number of regional Jobcentre plus offices where you can make direct contact with local advisers. For further details visit the website.

8. Open job applications
(be courageous)

Are you someone who does not wait until you are asked to do something? Would you rather hunt than be hunted? Then active jobhunting is something for you. And if you want to do this, you'd better first have the necessary background information about the companies – unless it does not bother you whether you work for the city of Manchester or the mafia. What is holding you back to consider possibilities abroad?

With an open job application you offer your services as jobhunter. There are three ways to do this. The first is to simply contact employers where you would like to work and which you know. (It is better to first telephone before you write a letter.) The second way is that you tell them about your qualities in an unsolicited letter and refer to new developments within the market place – and how your expertise and creativity can play an important role in the targeted company.

If it rains here, it may be pouring somewhere else, but elsewhere the sun will be shining. Investigating the labour market means that you find out where it is now sunny and experts forecast interesting economic growth, and you a golden future. This is the third way (easier said than done): you analyse and investigate a particular labour market, industry or organisation and study (foreign) trends, and come to the conclusion that company A is missing a particular sort of employee. Then you offer your services, which are very attractive to the employer.

9. Radio and television commercials
(notably unnoticed)
During economically strong times, recruiters like to make use of radio and television to flog their wares, their vacancies. These kinds of media are quickly dropped when the economy slows down. Do not expect too much in this area – until the labour market (or your chosen sector) picks up again. But it never hurts to keep your eyes and ears open.

10. Internships
(get your foot in the door?)
An internship can be a springboard to the next job. That includes completing an extra internship, a work experience project, a pseudo or voluntary internship. It comes down to getting a close up look at a certain position within a company for a predetermined amount of time (mostly one to six months). This has a number of advantages:

- You learn the profession (make sure that you are not put to work as an overqualified tea lady);
- It'll boost your confidence to 'be active', if you are currently unemployed;
- It looks good on your CV;
- You increase your network, both internally and externally – for instance suppliers;
- And maybe there is the chance – you have to get lucky once in a while – that you are offered a labour agreement.

The disadvantage is that you will not get one penny for your efforts. (At the very most your travel expenses will be reimbursed.) But in any case you are part of the company. This approach is also handy for a starter needing to get work experience.

11. Job fairs
(a walk through vacancy land or a puzzle derby?)

Visit job fairs, even when you are not part of the target group. The reason being that you will come in contact with the different recruiters at the fair. They probably also have other jobs in their portfolio than the ones they are promoting at the fair. If not, ask them about other job openings within their organisation (or at their clients) – and make an appointment to discuss them later on.

Also visit professional fairs which relate to your field. (Broaden your choice instead of narrowing it down.) Your goal is not to find out if the exhibitors have any immediate vacancies, but get a hold of them and ask (if need be sneakily) if there are 'possibilities' for someone like yourself in their company. Let them know that you are doing them a great service by introducing yourself, the ideal candidate, free of charge! There is a big chance that there are no positions at the moment. Do not despair. Perhaps they know of similar businesses which are considering hiring.

Besides the exhibitors, let's call them sellers, there are also buyers walking around. By approaching them, with a bit of luck, you may also come across potential jobs. Strike up a conversation while you are both standing in line for a cup of coffee.

12. Advertise yourself
(the opposite world)

Do not expect tremendous results when you advertise your services in a newspaper or trade journal, but since the costs may be low so why not give it a shot? First determine which 'product' you are offering and how you can get your message across. By using this method, you pay for the employer's recruitment costs. Thank you! Why would they not get in touch with you?

13. Other 'jobs' and contracts
(the alternative tour)
There are other possibilities to get back in the job market. Here are a few options:

- After making an investment (sometimes substantial, sometimes small) you can get down to business as a franchised entrepreneur.
- In a practice you own your own business but you share your general services and overhead with other members (for instance the reception, the lunchroom and meeting rooms). The big advantage is that the (start-up) costs can be minimal.
- With a freelance contract you can get to work. Your income is far from certain. However, if you can string enough of these contracts together you may be able to make a living.

(Refer also to Chapter 8.)

Jobs abroad
The world is a big place. You can consider countries where the economy is doing well, such as the oil rich and population poor Norway or an Asian country where there is a scarcity of some professions, such as China which has a great demand for pilots. What is holding you back from working abroad?

Jobhunting inside and outside the European Union
Do you hold a European Union passport? Then you have the right to work and live anywhere in the European Union. In other parts of the world it is more difficult, since you will need a work permit. Some foreign employers will be able to arrange the permit (especially if you have unique knowledge and skills). Many more will not be

prepared to do this and you will have to take care of that yourself. Keep this in mind before you send your resumé to job sites around the world.

There is a lot to consider when working abroad, such as the moving and other costs, children's schools, quarantine for the pets etc. Who is going to pay for that? (Something to negotiate with the employer.) Be aware that you have a stronger position with a European labour contract than in most countries outside the EU. And with only a vague promise or verbal agreement you may be in dire straits.

Reasons to work abroad

Why would you actually consider working abroad? Are you able to clearly explain your motivation to future employers or intermediaries, in writing or in a discussion? What attracts you? Is it just a whim or do you think you will spend the rest of your life in that country? Think first about what your reasons are, before you send out a job application abroad and before someone else asks you. You shall see that a strong, plausible answer is hard to come up with. And if you have to make a confession think of how you will react to these questions from the selection committee:

- What attracts you to work in (the country of your choice)?
- What are your less positive characteristics? What are your positive points? And what do you base your answer on? (Stress your flexibility and adaptability.)
- Do you have any earlier experience working abroad? (And what were your experiences?)
- Do you think you are independent? What has demonstrated this?
- How do you feel about being sent to one or more other countries?
- What do you bring to this (international) job? (Knowledge, insight, skills, language?)
- What do you think you will gain from this (international) position?

TIP

Selection specialists are trained to determine how strong your motivation is. They will eliminate the 'romantic' and the 'palm tree dreamer'.

!!!! DANGER !!!!

Consider the safety of the country or city when making your decision. The chances are that you will not reach your retirement if there are bullets flying past your ears.

Summary

Main points

1. It is not always easy to decipher the content of job vacancies. Realise that in most positions three tasks and/or responsibilities account for 80 percent of what you do at work. If the job vacancy text is not clear, call the contact.
2. There are many places where you can find job vacancies. Keep in mind that not all job openings will be found on the internet. Therefore, look further than the digital motorway.
3. Begin developing and building up your network long before you need it. Intensify this when you are looking for a (new) job.
4. There are different ways to do an unsolicited job application, depending on the energy you want to put into it. Pay attention to what *you* can offer the organisation.
5. Increase your search by considering the possibility of working abroad.

Worthwhile websites

Careerjet.co.uk	Worldwide job site
Allthejobs.co.uk	Mega job search engine
Freelancers.net	For freelancers looking for assignments.
Timeshighereducationco.uk	Job site for the higher educated
Jobrapido.co.uk	Mega job site (international)
Monster.co.uk	Worldwide job site
Direct.gov.uk/en/Employment/ Jobseekers	Government assistance for job-seekers, including Jobcentre Plus

If you have done all the necessary preparations, then we will help you in the following chapter to take action: contacting the employer. Slowly but surely you have to get out of your trench.

4

REACT:

WRITE, CALL AND MAIL

There are many different jobhunting techniques, but the one thing that you the (future) jobhunter need to remember all the time is to *sell* yourself, if you want to be seen as the ideal candidate. If *you* don't convince your counterpart, who will do that for you?

Your 'client', the future employer, will not only try to select the best candidate, but also to protect himself from future problems. Insurance companies do not offer policies for hiring the wrong people, so the employer has to take care of his own 'insurance'. This is comprised of at least three 'barriers' that you have to overcome: the application covering letter with curriculum vitae (CV), the job interview and finally the pre-employment assessment test.

In this chapter we will assist you to increase your chance of success, such as creating more contact moments with the employer, in order to show your interest. Writing an inspiring letter of application or motivation will be covered here as well. In short, we have arrived at the R in the KIRAP-CS of jobhunting. Time for action!

Quantity: one application letter every day

During an economic malaise, with murderous competition, you cannot afford to send an application letter every so often. (Except if you are one of those rare talents in your field.) We are not saying you should randomly dispatch your CV into digital space (the more, the better you would think), because that is like shooting a gun haphazardly, with a very small chance of hitting the target. We do advise to having a constant minimum production. For instance, mail out an average of one specific job application per workday. You can see right away if you have met your weekly criterion – and thus will know what to do next.

Suspicious employers

There is usually a grain of truth behind every rumour. That is why employers are so unsure and curious: what sort of person is hiding behind the application letter? What are his true characteristics? But sometimes they are paranoid or armed with a fresh dose of cynicism thanks to less positive experiences with new employees. What could this job applicant be *hiding*? Is he telling the truth? Is this a charlatan parading as a prominent internationally famous and respected experimental brain surgeon, complete with the slickest diplomas from non-existent foreign universities? Huge lies are hidden in the details.

What do job applicants hide?

- being unemployed (in the process of getting fired, on long-term sick leave, on or about to be put off-duty);
- missing the required diplomas and certificates (unfinished studies);
- a problem with drugs or alcohol (loss of one's driver's license);
- in a state of emotional turmoil (divorce, death of a family member);
- (day)therapy in a psychiatric hospital (now or in the past);
- having served a prison sentence;
- the size of their actual earned salary, the bonus, commissions etc;
- a serious financial problem (under legal restraint, in a debt restructuring programme).

Checklist: does your CV fit the job requirements?

You have a CV and a 'wanted' ad and you know what *you* want: this job! Based on the following points you can determine how closely your CV fits the listed requirements. Perhaps you will have to first adapt your CV, if you want to attract this employer's attention.

- Do you meet the verifiable requirements (education, work experience etc)? All of them? Most of them? (Check)

- Is there a logical line in your education and work career? Do they fit together?

- When did your career peak? And what did that mean to you? Or is that period still yet to come?

- Do your earlier acquired competencies fit the required competencies?

- Have you checked your CV for spelling errors or sloppiness? (These kinds of mistakes indicate inaccuracy, haste and disinterest.) This is deadly, particularly for jobs where precision or an eye for detail is called for.

- Would you describe your lay-out as attractive? Is it special? Does it stand out in the crowd?

- Are all your relevant extras in your CV? (Think of your language skills, foreign work or study experience, specific internship.)

- Are there any gaps (years or month), which indicate periods of 'doing nothing'?

- Do you list vague jobs or fake positions ('consultancy', 'freelance work', 'projects', work in the 'family business', 'interim assignment')? Beware of sharp recruiters.

- Will readers from outside your industry sector understand what your job titles mean? (If not, explain.) That also applies to the tasks and responsibilities.

- What does your CV suggest or imply (what overall 'message' does it send out)?

- Are there enough similarities between the tasks performed in your sector and the one you are aiming at?

- Have you stayed at your jobs for a short period of time (which implies job hopping, having made bad choices and/or being fired)?

- Do you have (sufficient) leadership experience, if that is what is asked for?

- Are your leisure activities realistic and robust? ('Skiing' means for most people one week per year, 'music' can be listening to your iPod in the train, everyone 'reads')

- What is the level of your language skills? If 'Italian' is on your CV, would you be able to converse with the Italian-born interviewer?

- Which facts back up your organisational skills? (Such as conventions, neighbourhood parties and study trips you claim to have organised.)

- Are all your memberships and board functions on your CV? (This indicates volunteering for your fellow man, community involvement etc.)

- Are there unfinished schools (left without a diploma), which could cause concern or difficulties?

- What is the *level* of your presentations delivered at business meetings or publications?

Five kinds of application letters

The primary goal of every application letter is to be invited for an interview. To reach that destination you should give the employer the requested information and present it attractively, 'with a bow'. While for most job seekers the letter is the first contact with an employer (or agent), we advise you to first grab the telephone and call. The advantages of this approach will be dealt with later in this chapter under 'Attracting attention: creating contact moments'.

There are five different kinds of application letters:

1. Open application letter
2. Letter of motivation
3. Traditional application letter
4. Reaction to a tip
5. Registering at a recruitment and selection agency, headhunter or interim agency.

If you know that the letter (reacting to an advertisement or an open application) is the first barrier, then you must invest the necessary time and energy. It is the first impression of yourself that you give. (Or the second, after your initial phone call, as mentioned before.) The application letter has several design and content aspects. It must look 'slick'. There has never been a job applicant that has gotten a job based only on the fairytale appearance of his letter, but a sloppy, hastily compiled letter (that gives the impression of being thrown together) will quickly land in the dustbin.

Being a business letter does not imply that it should have a neutral tone. *Enthusiasm* can be shown. The way that you describe yourself, and indicate what you could mean for the employer, says a lot about your *motivation*. Make it clear that you have done some *research* about your future position within the organisation.

TIP

Develop a 'job wish list' as soon as possible. What are you looking for in a job? Write that down in a few sentences and use it to assess every vacancy before your go or no-go decision. Although it is possible to look for a job as fast as a click on the internet, you may want to say 'no' if a job opening is too far removed from your ambitions.

1. Open application letter

An unsolicited job application was already described and 'sold' to you in Chapter 3. There are a number of reasons to write it. One is that after having done your personal research, you want to 'inform' an organisation about your expertise and enthusiasm. You focus in on a particular sector and want to approach one or more companies within that sector for a first frank and open discussion. The subjects which you choose could be the growth of the organisation, its products and services, its leading role in the sector, the fact that it is established near to your home, possibilities for personal development etc.

The big advantage of the open application letter is that when you contact an employer there will probably be no competition at that point in time. Furthermore, you can emphasise your qualifications and competencies, since there is (still) no concrete job description. With an open application letter, you show an active, entrepreneurial, enthusiastic you, someone who does not wait, but who creates opportunities.

2. Letter of motivation

Nowadays the letter of motivation is getting more and more attention. What does an employer want to read? Why you want to have *this* particular job and why in *this organisation*. Show them that you know and care about the company, the department and the described job responsibilities and why these fit you so well. You need to know which 'problems' you can solve for the employer, what your contribution will be, and what your added value is. That is different than reminding them how good this organisation fits into your career plans. The employer is not in the least interested in that. The reader is looking for the answer: what are my reasons for inviting this particular candidate for an interview?

Put *specific arguments* in your letter of motivation, focused on this employer and no other. It is obvious that British Airways is an internationally operating company, but that does not specifically apply only to B.A. Also think about what your 'hook' will be. That is the special, very creative (but not bizarre) point that has pushed you (into the arms of your favourite employer). Is it difficult for you to put your motivation in words, then maybe you are not so interested in this job. If so, stop this procedure. It'll be a complete waste of your and the employer's time.

If an **intermediary** asks for a motivational letter, then you will need to put in more *general* arguments.

3. Traditional application letter

Reacting to an advertisement is a stab in the dark, since you don't know how many other people reply. And even if you had that information, then it still does not do you much good. Some already published job vacancies are merely a formality. That happens when an internal candidate has been selected, but the organisation still is obliged to publicise all their vacancies. Or that the advertising space needs to be filled contractually, while there are no vacancies. A fake ad is better than a blank space, for the employer. That is why it is always wise to **first call** before you start writing.

It is important that your message is concise and powerful, because personnel managers and the other professionals who read application letters have little time and absolutely hate reading them. Your letter will be one of many. Limit it to one sheet of paper, and if you have a lot to say to a maximum of two pages. Keep in mind that 'quantity' is not always the same as 'quality'. Long letters are counterproductive: they irritate and are discarded.

It has to be clear from the very beginning that you are proficient in the position's tasks (or can learn them quickly) and why you want the job. The employer will not be impressed that you want to get **a** job, but why *this* job and why *with us*? (Make sure you show your *special interest*!) You need to know which 'problems' you can solve for your employer or which corporate challenges are right in your alley.

Point out that you have the necessary education and experience, required for successfully fulfilling this position. Perhaps you will have to show that, despite not having the required diploma, you are indeed well-qualified. It is also useful to demonstrate the development in your career path and how this job logically fits into this. The application letter is *not* a repeat of your CV. Avoid overlap between these two documents.

You have to convince them. How are you going to do that? The tone has to be positive and assertive: 'I have a lot of experience in... from my internship at factory X.' 'I am currently chairperson of the tenants' association Z, an active group that excels in ...' You have to get their interest: 'I lived for part of my youth in France, where my father was a correspondent for a British newspaper. (French is thus my second native language.)' The HR officer will start thinking: 'Hey, which paper would that have been?' 'Having someone on board who is fluent in French would be very handy for us.' In short, show them your best side. If you have special relevant skills and knowledge (that are not asked for in the job ad), then you will have to relate them to the position and emphasise them. This will give you an advantage over the competition.

You don't have to tell everything about yourself, since the interviews may be coming up. Seek a balance between enough information, being business-like and enthusiasm – put in a bit of each.

Examine your letters critically and ask yourself this question: why would they invite *me* to an interview?

4. Reaction to a tip

Via your personal network you have found out that a position might be coming up. That gives you the opportunity to react before the job vacancy is published, sometimes even before the job description has been written. Make reference in your letter, with his or her permission, to your contact person and the vacancy which he or she has told you about. You can sometimes ask for more information about the position, the company's culture and the person you hope to talk with.

5. Registering at a recruitment and selection agency, head hunter or interim agency

You can keep these letters quite general. The most important question is not what kind of person they are looking for, but: what can I offer or what am I looking for? Begin with a short introduction about the tasks that you have carried out, make reference to information in the attached CV. Then explain why you want to be in their file and what your preference is (sector, kind of position, which aspect of that position should be emphasised and perhaps an indication of your desired salary). Before you sit down at your computer to compose the letter, it is preferable to first call so that you know that you are contacting the correct party. And besides, in tough times many agencies are going out of business or have very few assignments.

Checklist: Application letter

Use this list as a starting point when writing your application letter or to check it afterwards.

Look and layout

- Choose the correct page layout (roomier margins are mostly more attractive) and a suitable letter font. Experiment with this. Adjust line spacing, letter size (11 to 12 points), and margins (left 3, right 2 centimetres) until you have found an attractive format.

- Are you sending a hard copy? Use somewhat distinctive writing paper, such as 'thicker' cream or light gray paper. (And set your printer for the best printing quality.)

- Your name and address must be mentioned. Design an attractive letterhead, for instance in the left hand corner, in another font. (Or give this task to a printer.)

- Name and address of the organisation, if necessary the department, are noted at the top. Under the address you write 'Re: ..... *(the specific vacancy)*'.

- Find out who you have to address in the letter ('Dear Mrs Campbell' or 'Dear Mr Lee').

- There must be a clear division of paragraphs, with the use of white space. The general rule is: one topic per section, for instance:
    - opening: begin the letter with a positive and specific remark about the company ('big challenge' is too general);
    - motivation to apply;

- interpretation of what is required: why you think you have the right competencies for it;
- what you 'offer' the reader: refer several times to your CV (but don't repeat items that are in there) and any attachments, as proof; point out you are willing to further qualify or to move, if that is relevant;
- closing: ask for an interview to further discuss your application.

- If there is something important that you want to emphasis. Do it (very sparingly) in **bold**.

Tone and language

- A varied use of words reads better. Don't put in the same words repetitively. (Consult a dictionary for synonyms or a thesaurus.) Make sure your spelling and punctuation are correct. Short and clear sentences are preferred, but be careful that your letter does not become too staccato, because that will make the reader fidgety (and your writing skills may be interpreted as poor).

- Do not sound too meek. While adhering to the normal rules of politeness make a proposal that is favourable for both you and the organisation.

- Likewise, don't be too boastful, arrogant or academic. Flaunting your persuasiveness, creativity or decisiveness, without backing these up with examples or hard facts, will result in rejection right away. Be aware that everything you claim must hold up during the interview! Even more important: *you* will be drawing attention to it.

- You will get their eyes with an original and specific motivation. Tell what makes the work interesting for you and why it *excites* you.

- In the letter's closing sentence, 'invite yourself' for a personal meeting, to get acquainted. It is only when you are there in person that you can convince others of your knowledge, abilities, skills, insight etc. The employer sees the 'car' – and it appeals to him. His next step will be a 'test-drive' to check it out (assessment tests).

- Limit the use of 'I' as much as possible. You cannot avoid it entirely, but if you play around with the sentence there is often another way to say the same thing. Use action verbs, such as 'led', 'supervised', 'wrote', 'achieved', 'developed'.

- The letter needs to have a logical structure and flow. The steps from one sentence to the next, from one paragraph to the next should not be surprising.

TIP

Most emails are full of mistakes. That is especially bad if your email is directed at a possible employer. Avoid this kind of sloppiness. Let a friend critically read your letter before you send it.

Contents of the letter

- React with what you have to offer and what is being asked for, so no paragraphs about your persuasiveness if it is only a paper pushing position. If you mention competencies or experiences that at the surface have nothing to do with the job description, make the connection. (The employer will not be impressed to hear you play the saxophone well.)

- Give information in a positive way. If you don't meet certain qualifications, do not mention them. You will be invited to an interview based on what you *can* do. If you miss a certain diploma, tell what you have done related to that area (and can compensate for this possible lack) or write that you are still studying for... and that you expect to have received your diploma by this date. Be realistic!

- If you are a structured person (or that is how you want to come across), then first make note of the requirements, in order of importance *to the employer*. Keep referring to them in your letter and offer some examples. You do not have to mention them all, only the most important ones. In this way you can downplay your weaknesses. If unclear, ask the HR officer or whoever is mentioned in the ad, which aspects of the job are the most important.

- You are motivated! (You do not have to use the word 'motivation.') Don't say you think the new position is 'interesting' (that is too commonplace), but make it clear that you have put a lot of thought in how you would perform in the job.

- There can be no negative reasons to apply. Don't mention that you are unhappy at your present job or currently unemployed – even if that is evident from your CV. Likewise, do not write that you would like to live in city A or in the north of the country. That is irrelevant, except for an unsolicited open application. You are applying because you are able to and want to make a contribution to this particular firm.

Example of a letter to an employer

E.A. Johnson
12 Dorset Street
Durham DH2 5TB

ABC
For the attention of Mr P. de Winter
P.O. Box 432
Manchester M1 3LB

15 May 2010

Re: Job vacancy 501 (Human Resources Manager)

Dear Mr de Winter,

As it was with more than general interest that I read your advertisement in *The Guardian* I immediately decided to telephone for more information about this position. The very pleasant conversation with Ms Nielsen has only increased my enthusiasm.

I feel very much attracted to ABC because they fulfil an important role in both society as a whole as well as in supporting individuals.

The policy to take real and powerful steps to decrease absenteeism at work due to sickness and disability (ABC has a considerably higher absenteeism than other associations of companies) appeals to me very much.

On the one hand I know that this problem must be solved by both the individual and society. On the other hand, reducing health-related absenteeism happens to be a part of my current job responsibility as a personnel manager at MBI in Henley. My contribution has been in the 'signalling' and prevention of absenteeism. We have been very successful with this approach. I shall gladly share the basis of this philosophy with you and how this method actually works.

Furthermore I have recruitment, selection and management support for labour conditions, salaries, training and education in my portfolio at the moment. I prefer well-rounded positions!

MBI is an excellent company to work for. Why then would I leave, you may ask. As you probably have read, there is a gigantic worldwide restructuring programme going on at the moment. Since 'tearing down' is the key word and I prefer to 'build up', I will eventually no longer feel at home at my current employer.

Considering my knowledge and experience, hands-on mentality, ability to work independently and the fact that I am also a great team player, I sense that a position as ABC HR Manager is the perfect job for me. I would be willing to relocate, if this position requires it.

In the attached CV you will find a short description with additional information about me. I would be happy to answer your questions in a meeting.

I look forward to your reply.

Yours sincerely,

(signature)

E.A. Johnson

Attachment: curriculum vitae

TIP

If you experience writer's block, or are not getting anywhere, take a walk, listen to music, sleep on it, study the behaviour of the ducks, ask a friend for help. The solution will present itself – don't force it.

The follow-up

It is common practice to receive a confirmation letter, but regrettably, that is not always the case. If you have not heard anything within two weeks (after the employer-set deadline), pick up the telephone or email. If it happens that you were not invited to an interview, then leave it at that. If you are 'being kept on file', contact again them in two weeks to see what the actual situation is. Be assertive!

Example letter to an executive searcher

E.A. Johnson
12 Dorset Street
Durham DH2 5TB

Eurosearch
Attn: Mr G.M. Brook
25 Panama Avenue
Glasgow G3 8SS

15 May 2010

Dear Mr Brook,

Within the near future I will be in the market for new employment. For the past four years I have had the position of trainer and consultant within a training agency. It is now time to broaden my horizons, acquire new experiences, search for new impulses.

As a part of my investigation of my possibilities, I would greatly appreciate the chance to have a meeting with you about what we could mean for each other. If I do not hear from you sooner, then may I take the initiative to call you next week to make an appointment?

For your information a copy of my CV is attached.

Yours sincerely,

(signature)

E.A. Johnson

Attatchment: CV

Achievements and competencies

You have to sell the most difficult product that exists: yourself. Emphasise your achievements in your accompanying letter, as long as they are *relevant* for the position you are eyeing, along with other personal characteristics that have led to these achievements (such as creativity, showing initiative and flexibility). Give clear-cut examples. Wherever possible put down exact figures to give your achievements body.

Competencies are in fashion! You see competency-based learning, competency-based leadership, competency-based selection, competency-based cigar label collecting and so much more. It is questionable if there is that much difference from the pre-competency era. What does 'competency' mean? Everyone has his own definition, but it all comes down to the idea that you need to have certain 'characteristics' to do a job successfully. Generally, this is seen as a combination of skills, knowledge, attitude, insight and motivation. Some organisations have compiled detailed competency handbooks, where all the positions have been broken down into competencies. Never mind that the overlap is often enormous. If the employer or intermediary starts talking about 'competencies', then do that as well.

Some personnel ads are completely clear; others remain as mysterious as Mona Lisa's smile (?) even after reading them 23 times. (Are they really trying to reach job seekers?) Now it is your turn: the employer that you are interested in may have indicated which competencies are necessary for this position. In your application letter you have to explain to which degree you possess these competencies and perhaps offer several short examples of them. Keep in mind, the letter has to be concise! Are you searching in the dark for which competencies are being asked for? Call and ask (= contact moment 1).

Attracting attention: creating contact moments

To increase your success, you will have to use all your tools (in a positive way) in order to set yourself apart from the competition. We advise you to create a large number of contact moments with prospective employers. (We are not talking about quantity here, these contact moments must be first rate.)

'What are the advantages of this extra effort?' you may ask.

1. You get your name known and make an impression.

2. The quality of your application letter improves, since you can better explain what attracts you to the position. And perhaps during the telephone conversation, you are the only one who gets inside information, which you can put in the letter. Maybe your astute hearing has picked up on company jargon destined for your application letter. You increase your chance to be accepted as OKP: Our Kind of Person.

3. You demonstrate with actions rather than cheap words how extraordinarily motivated and driven you are to get *this* job.

4. During the face-to-face interview you will know what you have to emphasis, which topics you need to bring up and which ones you should avoid. And show again how enthusiastic and motivated you are about the position ('The pleasant talk with you/Mrs Pearson/the HR manager'). And you can say great things about the organisation, the function and the person you had talked to, that both you and the interviewer know. Sharing knowledge helps creating a positive atmosphere.

The contact moments

Elevator pitch

Which contact moments are possible from the first time you catch sight of a suitable vacancy? Just be patient, first a side step, let's reflect on the *elevator pitch*. Imagine, you meet a VIP in a lift, and during the very short ride together you have to explain to him *who you are* and *what you want*. You have to accomplish this in a matter of seconds, before the VIP steps out. Do you have this pitch ready, even before your encounter begins? Do your homework, because you never know how much time the other person has for you. With a clumsy story full of umhs and ahs, hesitations and detours you will fail.

Contact moment 1

The first contact moment is the introductory telephone call. As soon as you have drawn the conclusion that this is 'your' job, grab the telephone and talk to the contact person mentioned in the advertisement. Because you *always* need more specific information about the organisation and/or job. If no contact person nor telephone number in the ad is to be found, call up (every organisation can be reached by telephone) and ask who the best person would be to approach with your burning questions (such as: 'What does the average day of this employee look like?'). Your sound bytes for the lift pitch will come in handy if your telephone partner is busy, busy, busy.

There is a disadvantage attached to an introductory talk: you may get interrogated by an impatient person, so that you can't put your best foot forward. Keep it in mind: your aim is to get extra information about the company and **not** have a job interview. If you want to talk with a helpful and motivated person, forget Monday morning and Friday afternoon. The best times to call are between 9:30 am and 11:30 am and between 2:00 pm and 4:00 pm. If these times are still not favourable, ask when it would better to call. Your perseverance will pay off!

Contact moment 2

You write and send the (digital) application or motivation letter, along with the CV and any attachments.

Contact moment 3

A few days later, you email a short note to your contact person. You report, for instance, that you have found an interesting article on the internet or in a (foreign) newspaper or magazine. You say that you suspect that this employer has not seen this news item yet.

Alternatively, you can tell them that you had forgotten to write something in your letter of motivation...and it would be good to pass on that...

Contact moment 4

The fourth contact moment is that long awaited meeting, the job interview, which you have lobbied for in your correspondence.

Contact moment 5

Right after the interview, you send a letter in which you first thank them for the pleasant and open discussion. You *always* add something, for example something that you noticed during the company tour... Or you offer a suggestion, based on similar experiences from another employer. You are going *very* far if you submit a one page report containing several strong pieces of advice.

Contact moment 6

You are very assertive if you contact the employer again ('Say, what is happening with that job!?') It could be seen as pushy and that can be dangerous. If you think that it is time to take action (last attempt), then send something that is interesting to the employer. And we are not talking about a box of cigars.

Telephone script skills

If you happen to have a telephone-phobia, keep two things in mind:

1. Is this job worth so little that I will not improve my chances?
2. What is the worst that can happen if I call? (What do I have to lose? My house? My stamp collection? My boat? My life?)

By composing a script, you will be able to overcome your fears, become calmer and not be thrown off kilter by any over-confident person. On top of that, the effectiveness (improved dialogue) of your telephone call will increase enormously. Due to this preparation you will be able to get your point across in a relatively short time. If necessary, use the following form, before jumping into the deep end.

Telephone script form (fill in yourself)

Goal(s) of this discussion:

Example: Be invited for a personal meeting in the short term, by a headhunter.

How am I going to introduce myself, opening words:

Example: 'My name is Jane Doubleincome and I am ready for a new step in my career. Do you have time right now or should I call back later? Which date and time would suit you better?'

Career goals:

Example: 'My goal is to become financial manager of a small organisation, where I can also be part of the management team.'

Why I have approached this manager or headhunter:

Example: 'I found the name of your agency in the ABC recruitment and selection guide and I understand that you specialise in positions with salaries above £75,000.'

Attractive strong points (knowledge, skills, achievements) that I will mention:

Example: 'You have most likely heard of the Stop-pain ad campaign. This campaign was not only awarded the Golden Lamp. It also led to an increased turnover of 33 percent. The basic concept was my creation and I contributed to its further development. Is that of interest to you?'

My work experience:

Example: 'I have been an accountant for a midsize accountancy firm for about three years.'

Be careful with how you use 'have been'. It could be interpreted that you have already left the company.

Questions I would like to ask:

Example: 'Do you have vacancies for people of my calibre on a regular basis?'

My closing statement (including the thank-you):

Example: 'Thank you for your time. I will send you my CV right away, as I am even more enthusiastic about the position we discussed. I hope that I will be invited for an interview soon so I can explain what I could mean for the Turned On Energy Corp.'

What to do if the discussion stagnates:

Example: 'It is probably interesting for you to know that I have worked intensively with the current chairperson of the Project Developers Association for many years.'

Telephone tips

1. Think of what you want to say *ahead of time*. Improvise as little as possible. But do not become a telephone robot with the flat, bored and cold voice of someone working through a list of questions, like call-centre agents and salespeople.

2. Concentrate on the telephone conversation and don't do other things at the same time (like reading the newspaper, playing with your pen, looking through your email, analysing how Wall Street is doing, drinking, chewing, smoking or doing the washing up).

3. What is the very least that you want to achieve with this telephone call? What is your goal? For example, arranging an interview or submitting your CV.

4. Compose a list of the points that, regardless of what else happens, you want to bring up and keep this within reach. That could also be certain characteristics that you see as your strengths.

5. Keep a pen and paper ready for making notes during the call.

6. Don't give away everything, but save some information for a later interview. Make the other person curious (with a teaser), for instance like the telephone script interview for the Stop-pain advertising campaign, so that you will get invited for a meeting.

7. Try to explain in *one minute* which tasks and responsibilities characterise your own position. Name the tasks in order of importance or amount of time. Describe abstract responsibilities as concretely as possible.

8. Make sure that you are feeling good about yourself. If you are depressed or do not have enough drive, the other person will quickly pick up on that. If you do not believe in yourself, who will then?

9. Adjust the speed of your speech to the other person. Nervous callers often talk fast; in that case, lower your tempo.

10. Do not get thrown off balance by someone who acts important or is not approachable.

Overqualified

If you have an extra diploma or interesting foreign work experience, you could have an added advantage. But it could also work against you. That is what is employers call being 'overqualified'. If an interviewer tells you you are overqualified, what does this mean?

It could be a white lie. The idea being that the shot-down candidate will rather feel better with a compliment than a straight out rejection ('You are one of the best candidates that we have seen!' And then your qualities are closely examined and you get all kinds of praise. Yes but...).

Other reasons for labelling someone as overqualified:

- The employer is afraid that you will quickly get bored – and so will quit. (Adios investment.)
- That the difference (knowledge, skills, experience, studies) between you and the troops is so big that communication between the two parties is doomed to fail.
- The employer does not want to deal with your possible constant criticism of the organisation and the desire to improve situations.
- The (preconceived) idea that your remuneration demands are too high. (Above budget, or not in line with the salaries of the colleagues.)

TIP

Make it a habit to see something positive in every misfortune (rejection). Look for that silver lining in every cloud: a learning experience, a springboard for a new insight, a chance to do things entirely different, you as a Madonna (the singer) being reinvented all over again.

Summary

Main points

1. Be productive: send off at least one application per day.
2. Check how interesting vacancies match your profile. Use the checklist 'Does your CV fit the vacancy?'.
3. There are five kinds of application letter; each one requires a different approach. The required motivation letter is just a specific application letter.
4. Beware of the speed of digital jobhunting, resulting in unwanted mistakes in your documents.
5. If you want to stand out from the competition, then create a number of contact moments.

Worthwhile websites

Aperfectcv.co.uk	Tips for application covering letters
Jobsearch.about.com	Application letters and CVs
Jobs.startpage.co.uk	A starting point for many websites with application letters and other career tools

The next chapter will deal with the necessary administration of the jobhunting process.

5

ADMINISTER:

MAKING AND MANAGING LISTS

You want a job – and fast! Unfortunately, you will seldom find that desired position after only one try. If it is necessary to apply for jobs all over the place, and for a longer period of time, you will want to – no, you must – have some kind of system. Otherwise, at a certain moment, you won't see the forest from the trees. During an interview it becomes embarrassingly painful if you can't remember which version of your CV the selection committee has.

We are now at the fourth step (A), which carries on throughout your job search. We will focus on how to organise all your jobhunting information and activities; the administration is tedious and takes time, we know. That's why we offer help and cover a number of related concerns.

Making lists

In Chapter 2 we have already advised you that, along with a standard CV, a number of 'specialised' (adjusted) CVs will increase your chance of success. It is important that you keep records of the particular resumés you have sent out. Don't let this slip, because you run the risk of stumbling over a 'CV question' during an interview, since you forgot about that particular version.

If your search is primarily limited to 'visiting headhunters' and you want to keep them up to date on a regular basis, then this will quickly grow out of proportion. Just do the maths: forty headhunters times one contact moment per month – do you remember who you spoke to about what after three months?

We have already advised you to telephone to find out about a suitable vacancy and at the same time to get ammunition for your application. Perhaps you have an excellent memory, perhaps not... Therefore, you need to make a short record of the call. Who did you speak to? On which date? What did you both agree on? Which steps will be taken next? Combine this with the other jobhunting activities in order to see at a glance (handy for unexpected telephone calls from recruiters) exactly what the situation is, so you can quickly react. Use a list such as the one below and save it in a text, spreadsheet or database document.

Employer, intermediary (website)	Telephone contact with: .... Date: .... Initiated by:	Summary discussion	Appointments made/ steps to be taken	Make contact on: .... with:	Version CV	Topics discussed
A						
B						
C						

For a sound administration put all your papers into a plastic folder: all the originals, including the advertisement you have reacted to, your application letter, a copy of the employer's website, all correspondence and telephone notes. Store all these files in your jobhunting binder, so that you will always have all the information at your fingertips.

The evidence portfolio

Another kind of administration is collecting documents from past activities. Photographers do it, advertising copywriters do it, journalists do it, so why not you? Make a portfolio which shows evidence of your diverse initiatives, creative solutions and discoveries. You can get a plastic portfolio case for about £10 at any stationary shop.

What do you put in this evidence binder? Any proof of accomplishments. You can make a digital overview, but it is still advisable to have something tangible to give the interviewer. (Whether he reads these pieces is of less importance.) For example, put in a copy of the brochure for the study trip to Hungary that you thought up and organised. Or the letter from the club's chairperson, thanking you for your outstanding contribution. A critical observation during a holiday job resulted in large savings for the company; an article about this, with your photo, in the company's magazine says a lot about who you are. Published articles that you have written for a newspaper or (trade) magazine are great examples of your initiatives – no-one held a gun to your head. And it goes without saying that you are creative! Have you been a speaker at a congress or a seminar? Then it would be easy to find proof of that. Have you received a thank-you note from the highest boss in your organisation? Or is there a photo with both of you? There you go, in the file! Think about diverse situations like programme books where your name appears, 'key-memos', project plans (summaries), building plans, acknowledgements, references from ex-employers, membership cards etc. Have you named a certain accomplishment in your letter and/or CV (such as an increase in customer satisfaction by 10 percent); put the evidence (letter from the director, a page out of the report where the figures and your name appears) in your portfolio. What should also be in the file: the correct CV and all your diplomas, awards and certificates. Then you will have these at hand, if need be. Do not hesitate to **adjust** your portfolio for the position which you have an interview for. Your life in one file.

New job categories are continually being created; 'old' jobs disappear – permanently. No matter how much work can be automated or sent abroad, there will always be a need for thinkers, visionaries, thought provokers, and exceptional doers. Every organisation will always be interested in those people who are just that little bit more creative, who take initiative and who get the most done. Are you that kind of person? Is there proof of that in your portfolio?

The experience matrix

Imagine, your work experience at many different employers varies widely. In order to present this in an overview (for future employers, intermediaries, whoever), it is handy to table this information and put this in your portfolio. Be careful not to lose focus. Compare your scheme to the three most important tasks of a position that you want to get, as is described in Chapter 3.

	Kind of experience		
	Sales to retailers	*Sales to wholesalers*	*Sales management*
Employer/sector			
De Winter & Greenspan (bicycles)	2 years		
Ansary (paper import)		3 years	
Dal-gic (cigars)		2 years	1 year

You can fill in more information per cell. Make sure you won't lose the overview.

References

Employers have a fast and cheap way (one telephone call) to validate your story. Have you indeed worked for the landscaping company 'The Orange Carnation' for three years? They will contact your ex-boss, which you have given as a reference. Here are the important points you need to keep in mind:

1. It goes without saying that you have asked the referees' permission to be contacted.
2. You let them know that they can expect a telephone call within three days from Mr A from company B. (Perhaps you can also 'advise' them what should be said to Mr A...)
3. You never offer references spontaneously; only if the other party asks for them. (Don't put them on your CV either.)
4. Pass on these names, positions and telephone numbers in the last stage of the selection procedure.
5. Give the future employer or agent (verbal) permission to get in touch with your references. Ask them to do that in a few days, so that you have some time to talk to them first.
6. Showing reservations about giving references will make the other person suspicious. What are you hiding? What is the real story?

TIP

Be thrifty with your references. When your spokesperson has been bothered seventeen times within three weeks, his enthusiasm about you will quickly wane.

An alternative to the verbal reference would be to get a letter of reference from current or former employers. In general, recruiters don't value these very much. They know that the candidate will only collect those positive epistles – which may be choked out of employers during a legal procedure, or forged: written by oneself on the former boss's stationary.

A few examples of questions during a telephone reference check:

- What was your exact relationship with…?
- When exactly has he been employed by you? And what was the position(s)?
- What was the reason for his departure (at the moment or previously)?
- Which kind of evaluations did he receive (over the years)?
- How many sick days has he had per year (over the years) ?
- What do you find the most positive about him? (And why?) And the most negative?
- Would you hire him again? (Why or why not?)
- Our candidate states that he earned a gross salary of £3,500 per month. Can you confirm that?

What do you do if the future employer is emphatic about speaking with 'your current employer', while you slammed the door behind you a while ago or you are no longer on the payroll? That is a dilemma, since you have told a different story about your present-day work. Do you keep the fairytale alive or is it time to confess?

The weekly activity scheme

Work structures life, and that falls apart when you are out of a job, making disciplined jobhunting difficult. If this pertains to you, it can be useful to make a scheme wherein you set down a regular pattern of daily obligations and tasks. It goes without saying that looking for a job is your number one priority, followed by sport and leisure.

	Monday	Tuesday	Wednesday	Thursday	Friday	Weekend
Morning	Jobhunting	Sport	Jobhunting	Jobhunting	Jobhunting	
Afternoon	Reading, keep up to date with trade literature	Jobhunting	Professional meeting	Networking (lunch)	Networking (lunch)	
Evening	Keeping own blog up to date	Networking, watching TV	Going out	Sport	Going out	

All the aspects of looking for a job fall under 'jobhunting' (visiting websites, going for interviews, making tests etc). The scheme from Chapter 3 about searching job sites can be integrated into this plan.

Ethics and jobhunting codes

Job seekers have no specific rights like employees and tenants have. There is some protection via the code of ethics applied by several professional associations, which members (recruiters and selectors) must abide by.

By ethics we mean the formal code of conduct in which a professional group prescribes how its members must act. Just to be clear: only registered members can be brought before their internal 'court' if there is an offence. In the recruitment and selection arena codes of ethics apply for psychologists, personnel managers, and personnel recruiters.

No reaction? Rejected?

Heard nothing yet?

What does the assertive and effective jobhunter do if there is only silence from the employer or intermediary after the interview? (That may be impolite, but it still happens.) He first thinks and then takes action.

1. Perhaps you are on the reserve list, until they have reached an agreement with their intended *numero uno*.
2. Maybe the decision-maker or an important influential is sick or on holiday, so that the procedure has come to a standstill.
3. All kinds of business situations, which have nothing to do with you, could also play a role.

If you were told that you would hear something within a week and that period of time has elapsed, then make a call yourself. Do not accuse them ('You had promised to...'), but show understanding.

Rejected by letter

What if you have been rejected and all has been for nothing? Should you email them back? No. *Call.* You have nothing to lose and everything to gain. Maybe your rejection was a mistake. Do not assume that, but it has occurred that candidates have been switched. You want to find out during the telephone call why you have been rejected and/or get suggestions to improve your next move. With some luck you will get a tip about contacting company X, where they are also looking for someone like you. You will never learn about that, if you creep into your shell after having received the bad news.

Summary

Main points

1. For serious jobhunting you need a lot of contacts. Make sure you set up an administrative system otherwise you will quickly lose track.
2. Build up a portfolio with evidence ahead of time, which you can take to interviews.
3. Employers and intermediaries may ask you for references. Lay the groundwork early on.
4. You do not have any special legal protection as a jobhunter. There are codes of ethics for members of various professional association's (recruiters, psychologists, management consultants). This may offer some comfort during the interview.
5. If you have been rejected, following an application letter or interview, make a follow-up call so that you can do a better job presenting yourself next time.

Worthwhile websites

Iacpr.org	International code of ethics for executive searchers and similar professions
Cipd.co.uk	Code of ethics for employers (compiled by personnel employees)
Bps.org.uk	Code of ethics for British psychologists

Research is the subject of the next chapter. We'll discuss collecting information on employers, jobs and much more.

6

PREPARE:

RESEARCH THE EMPLOYERS, THEIR JOBS AND GO FOR THE INTERVIEW

This is the chapter for the researchers, control freaks and those who do not want to leave anything to chance. You have already done the necessary homework, before you sent your application or motivation letter out the door and hope to be invited for an interview. In between you can't afford sitting like a zombie, during these less booming times. The perfect job application demands (even more) research, research, research. Prepare yourself until the most miniscule detail, because that will guarantee you results (not per se with your first application).

We will pay special attention to the group of young people, starters, without work experience, that have to deal with particular problems. This chapter will provide you the ammunition to face that feared audition. Chapter 7 elaborates further on that trial called the job interview.

Prove that you are perfect for the job

At the interview with a potential employer, you hope to demonstrate that you fit together like Romeo and Juliet, but then without the tragic ending. Before it gets that far, you will be grilled with a rain of prying questions. Perhaps at a certain moment during this interrogation you may not come up with the right answer and lose the (chess) game. Game over. A solid preparation for an interview thus becomes a bitter necessity.

If you, driven by fear and uncertainty, make a mental sketch of your opponent, then you may get the wrong image of him, resulting in negative reactions. When you approach the interviewer as a potential *friend*, as someone who has the best intentions (and time and energy) for you, the generated *positive atmosphere* will increase your chances.

Failure factors

Several years ago, American HR managers were interviewed to find out which (simple) characteristics they paid attention to, as to quickly eliminate unfit job applicants. The result was a list of about forty items, called failure factors, which job applicants must *not* have or show. Here they are:

1. Poor personal grooming.
2. Overly aggressive, superior, know-it-all attitude.
3. Weak communication skills, poor voice, weak grammar.
4. No career plan, no goals, no direction.
5. Lack of interest or enthusiasm, passive, indifferent.
6. Too little self-confidence, nervous, not comfortable.
7. No social activities (clubs, team sports etc).
8. Emphasis on money, only interested in the best paid jobs.
9. Full of excuses about unfavourable situations in their past (employment).
10. Not tactful.
11. Impolite, ill-mannered.
12. Angry, speaks negatively about former (current) employer.
13. Lack of social skills.
14. Not energetic.
15. No eye contact with interviewer.
16. Soft, clammy hands.
17. Indecisive.
18. Lounging around and being lazy during holidays.
19. Poor marriage.
20. Sloppily filled in application form.

21. Is not keeping his options open.
22. Wants a job (for a short time) and not a career.
23. Poor sense of humour.
24. Little (factual) knowledge within his specialty.
25. No interest in the employer or its sector.
26. Emphasis on the people the candidate knows (acquaintances above knowledge).
27. Not willing to move or travel a lot.
28. Cynical, ironic.
29. Low moral values.
30. Lazy.
31. Intolerant, strong prejudices.
32. Few interests.
33. Biggest hobby: passive pastimes (like watching TV).
34. Poorly managed personal income.
35. No interest in activities and developments in the community or society at large.
36. Cannot take criticism.
37. Does not learn from his experiences.
38. Radical ideas.
39. Arrives at the interview too late, without a sound reason.
40. Has not researched the company ahead of time.
41. Does not ask any questions about the job.
42. Excitable personality ('problem maker').
43. Answers questions vaguely.

Now you know – almost – all the things you could be judged on. You have been warned, so be careful!

Googling your interview partners

Nowadays it is very easy to find the birth certificate of your interrogator(s) before you go to the audition. With a little investigative work (in this case via LinkedIn), an active jobhunter found out that his potential American boss was a water polo fan, according to his published CV. Talking about this sport resulted in a relaxed mood during the interview. (Regrettably, he did not get the job because his Spanish wasn't fluent.) Make it a habit to do 'biographical research' on your interrogators.

One chance to get it right

You will get many chances to screw up the interview. That is not so hard to do... It is, of course not a major problem when the job interviews are lined up for you. In reality, most jobhunters have to be satisfied with only a few appointments. It would be sad to discover that you are being rejected due to your own unnecessary blunders. Do not mess it up for yourself, not even if the interviewer happens to be quite a jerk. Act as if you are used to handling situations like this one. Think of the 'trump card' you will play out during the interview.

A permanent (positive) impression during the interview

Politely answering questions is simply not good enough, the same applies to being a yes-(wo)man and agreeing to just about everything. You will be in trouble (unknown to you) if ten minutes after you have left the audition, the interviewer only has a vague, fuzzy notion that he had a visitor, but can't remember who he talked to. A few tips to make sure the interviewer does not forget you so easily:

- Give answers containing the necessary professional terminology.
- Ask appropriate and sharp questions, which the other person has to think about. Poor candidates don't ask questions.
- Ask a number of critical questions about the organisation and the position.
- Make it somewhat difficult for the other person to sell the position to you. (But not too difficult, of course!)

- Explain that you are further along in discussions with other organisations (recruitment and selection agencies). This is not illogical for a jobhunter; and besides, you will not be the employer's only candidate during the first round of interviews.

Dress code

Regarding recommended clothing, we can be very concise:

1. Wear clothes which are normally worn where you want to work. If you are clueless find out: via your network or the network of your network or stand by the entrance of the business and observe how people are dressed.
2. Choose formal over informal. A neat business suit, but not too snazzy.
3. Cover any obvious piercings or tattoos, since these are not appreciated everywhere.

The job interview will also go better if you do not have bad breath.

Age discrimination

It is legally forbidden, but in job-hunting-land age discrimination is very prevalent. A few examples.

- A 21-year-old solicitor cannot find a job because he is too young. 'Go and get some life experience first,' suggests the personnel manager. With reason?
- A 37-year-old woman has written hundreds of letters to employers. Too bad. They are all looking for someone between 25 and 35. Are you old and worn out at age 37?
- The 60-year-old unemployed manager is laughed at. At that age you should be relaxing, doing volunteer work or play golf.

During poor economic times older people are victimised; their application letter will be subtly shoved to one side. And if they call for an explanation, the message is that their experience does not fit the 'profile', or some other similarly vague phrase. (A few intermediaries will allude to the fact that their clients have a problem with the candidate's age. Along with the threat: 'You have not heard this from me!') You could drag the employer to court, but obtaining credible evidence is quite another matter, and you can kiss that employer goodbye.

If you are invited for an interview, despite that age hurdle, what is the best approach?

1. Emphasise what your knowledge and experience, built up over the years, can mean for the employer.
2. Point out the strong network that you will bring with you.
3. If the employer starts talking about your age (which he has surely seen on your CV), ask why this is that important. Is it not your expertise and experience that counts? If it has to do with costs (without batting amounts back and forth like a ping pong ball), describe your flexibility and willingness to invest in yourself (read: willing to take a lower salary). You have a low mortgage and the children have flown the coop; your spending patterns are manageable. It is, of course, practical to get an indication of the salary to be offered before you get too enthusiastic...
4. You are not a job-hopper and will remain loyal to the company, through good and bad times. You don't have the urge to backpack through Australia for half a year.
5. You will not be distracted by family responsibilities and young children.
6. You know yourself well, are resolute and can better assess risks and chances.

Naturally, it helps if you have self-insight. Is the organisation looking for a 'young and dynamic' team player? And you are not so chirpy and somewhat slow. Then, aside from you age, you will not make the cut. Ouch!

What to do after the interview

Does the game stop (for the time being) after the interview, until the results are known? You can do your administration (Chapter 5) and make neat and colourful statistics. That it interesting and it will give you a feeling of being busy. But there is a better way to use your time, considering the fact that you have not been rejected yet and the race is still on.

Take action so that, again, the employer pays attention to you. Consider creating a contact moment (refer to Chapter 4). Furthermore, keep yourself in view of headhunters and recruiters. Stay active and do not put all your eggs in one basket.

Building blocks for the job interview

You do not have to divulge everything about yourself during an interview. This is *your* interview! You can steer it too. Think ahead about which bridges you wish to cross to get to the topics you want to discuss (such as strong points and important experience). Paint an image which marketeers call a competitive advantage.

Knowledge = motivation: do your research

According to many: knowledge is power. But during your job hunt, knowledge stands for motivation. What we mean is that the selection expert sees **your** knowledge of **his** (client's) organisation as a measure of your motivation. The candidate that has sent out 83 job applications and had 4 invitations to interviews in the last month, cannot dig into all these (83 or 4) organisations. If you limit yourself to a few possible interviews, then you *will* have the chance to do extensive research.

You will score when you are knowledgeable about the company you apply to. Show it by remarks like:

- 'In your last annual report I read that...'
- 'In the sector overview it said that your market share in Southeast Asia has gone up.'

- 'Your proposed merger with Combinier was stopped. Why was that exactly?'

The more a jobhunter knows (can tell) about the employer, the easier the interview flows. The result: a connection will be built up with the interviewer.

So, knowledge equals motivation. But you will have to get this knowledge from somewhere. Where do you look?

- The internet is naturally the ten lane motorway that you will drive onto right away: just google for free annual corporate reports, industry reports, 'newspaper articles' and press releases about the organisation you are interested in. Also, if relevant, check the stock prices, with any added analysis from stock exchange analysts and financial experts.
- Look for help in the trade journals (editors). Call, if necessary.
- Do you want to work for a bank or chain store? Visit a number of sectors, make notes and possibly do a photoshoot of the interior and exterior. And test: open a bank account, buy something at a shop.
- Expand your knowledge via acquaintances and through informal circles. Ask people to introduce you to their relations, who happen to know someone working at the ABC Bank. (This person could inform you about the company's culture, the dress code, rules and other practices.)

The more you know, the smarter your questions will be and the more tactical your answers. You can never know enough.

Your added value

Think about it ahead of time: large amounts of money will be put on the table to get you to join the company. Starting from your first day of employment, you will cost money (and perhaps also cause problems). But what will you contribute (in the long term)? In other words: what are you bringing to the table? What is your added value? What would happen if you did not accept this position?

Would the organisation go on operating or would important bottlenecks and problems occur? Does it really matter to the employer if you join the company? If you cannot think what *you* will contribute, then sooner or later you will have a problem – and probably sooner than later.

Answering questions: the analytical approach

Great answers are often reactions that have been analytically constructed. What do we mean? Firstly, you have broken down an idea into its most important parts. Then you have named and clarified them. For example, the question is: 'What do you think about being a supervisor in the near future?' Your answer: 'There are a number of aspects of supervising. I think that the (three, five) most important... I would like to explain, one by one, how I would deal with these aspects on the work floor.'

General speaking, this approach shows insight and conviction. But it will be necessary when the employer is looking for an analytically-gifted thinker. The following scheme will give you some guidance:

Tasks (responsibilities)	My abilities	'Evidence' (experience) verbal or written
1.		
2.		
3		
4.		
5.		
6.		
7.		

Explanation

Step 1. Break down the position into a number of tasks. (Look at the job description or the job ad.)

Step 2. For each task, describe which experience you have had in that field or which knowledge you possess.

Step 3. Perhaps the interviewer will trust the answer, but most probably he will want to test a few of the cited experiences: present evidence (written documents or oral examples).

If you are asked if you *can* do something (abilities), do not say that you *would like to* do it (motivation), because that is not a suitable answer and a foregone conclusion.

Questions you are going to ask

You will have the best job interview ever, you have already decided that. Although you are occupying the 'hot seat', there are also topics that *you* want to bring up. You do that to find out if the company suits you, but also to show you have studied this employer thoroughly. Which questions do you want to ask your host/hostess – as far as the answers are not known?

- How big is the organisation (in terms of employees and turnover)?
- Is this company profitable?
- What is the company's reputation?
- Is there a mission statement and what is it?
- What are the plans (for the coming x years)?
- Are any big changes expected (for example a merger, takeover or split up of the company)
- Are there plans to move the premises?
- What is the relationship with the parent company (or subsidiary)?

- Are there specific training programmes (business courses, management trainee programmes, management development programmes, crash courses)?

The bigger the organisation, the more information you can expect. Also ask *progress questions*:

- What is the next step (round) in this selection process? Will that be internal or external?
- Is there a (formal) introductory programme? If so, what does it look like?

TIP

You have 'asked for' the job interview, so it is impossible that you don't have any questions. Make a list and take this to the interview. Remember to carry a notepad with you, for writing down crucial answers.

Smiling is allowed

You may think that you always have to make serious and/or wise remarks and look intelligent. Laughing is absolutely allowed. Humour and anecdotes are great tools, but it is just like drinking alcohol: use moderation.

Adjust your voice to the other person's

Your voice can sometimes betray you. Therefore, it is important that your voice works as a sales tool during the job interview. A powerful voice belongs to a powerful personality (that is how it is interpreted). A loud voice is seen as assertive (that is favourable), but that also gives the impression that you are brash or hard of hearing (that is unfavourable). A shaky or trembling voice will imply fear or uncertainty, while a flat and monotone voice is associated with a boring, disinterested or uninteresting person. Talking quickly shows enthusiasm, intelligence and assertiveness. Do not talk so slow that the North Pole is melting in the meantime.

Be flexible

Sometimes meetings take unexpected turns. Imagine, you have applied for a certain position and at the end of the interview you are asked if you would be prepared to be a trainee for the company (for a period of half a year or a year). How do you react to the proposal? Do you agree right away or do you ask for time to think it over? Or do you start talking about its pros and cons?

Motivation, *enthusiasm and passion*

The motivation for your profession can be found in how you originally chose your study or vocation. Which aspects were important for the decision you made? If it was primarily your parents that influenced you, for instance because they thought at the time that the profession offered great opportunities, that says too little about *your* intrinsic motivation. Or it says a lot about it...

'I am only looking for a job, it comes down to having to pay my rent/mortgage every month,' is not a convincing argument (however true it may be). The future employer or intermediary wants to know that you really want *his* job. If that is not the case, because you barely see a future together and your stay will be limited, then fake it. Show that spark, be energetic. If the interviewer is incredibly proud of the gilded paperclips that they developed a few years ago, then you must not only imagine that it is terrific. You recognise the importance of it for all of humanity and tell how much you would like to help to make this utterly unique product a hit.

The discussion with the interviewer has to be logical and rational, but with some emotion added. 'Great dancers are not great because of their technique, but because of their passion,' stated dance legend Martha Graham. At an appropriate moment explain what *your passion* for this work is. You don't have to be dramatic, but being passive is like a kiss of death. Be dynamic (use gestures, move), show proof that you are energetic. If you are asked what you do in your free time, then you are definitely not a couch potato; you take adventurous holidays. Your voice is excited (high tones, faster speed – but not too fast) and positive words and adjectives make your story powerful and interesting.

TIP

If it costs you a lot to get excited about the employer and/or his products (but you need this job), keep something in mind that interests you, perhaps a hobby or holiday plans.

The STAR-method

Modern interviewers like to interrogate job applicants with STARs, since they want to learn something concrete about the applicants' behaviour in specific situations. If you are aware of this, you can train yourself. It is a simple model:

- What was the exact **S**ituation?
- Which **T**asks were you responsible for?
- Which **A**ction(s) did you take?
- What was the **R**esult (were the results) of the action?

This STAR for a starter: 'I was a member of a somewhat inactive student association (S) and had the task (T) as a member of the activity committee to develop new initiatives. From a needs analysis, which I carried out under members (A), it became apparent that there was an interest in inviting a guest speaker to the first meeting of every month. I successfully organised that programme. I signed on compelling guests and the membership participation doubled that year! (R)'

Who's to blame for your dismissal?

If you have been fired by your last employer, or a previous one, then painful questions may arise. It is important to look at the difference between just and unjust dismissals. It is *your fault* when you are constantly under-performing, show consistently unacceptable behaviour, have a vision that is completely incompatible with the top of the organisation, have eloped the boss's daughter etc. It is *not your fault* when your company has filed for bankruptcy, or is being taken over. A merger, reorganisation, downsizing or the loss of a subsidy can lead to involuntary holidays.

Specifics for starters

Brand new members of the labour market will sometimes underestimate the importance of the job interview, or put too much emphasis on it, showing interview anxiety. What are the specific problems?

- No (relevant) work experience (Logical.)
- No idea why an employer would want to offer him or her a job.
- Not realising that a job is an investment, for both parties, from the first day of work on.
- Not seeing oneself as an 'economic' commodity.
- Unsure about one's capabilities (possesses mostly 'paper knowledge', supplemented with an internship – for whatever that is worth).
- Unsure about one's financial worth.
- No interview experience.
- Maybe too little to report.
- Not aware that something has been achieved with the study.
- No idea how to 'sell' volunteer work, board functions, and other positions inside and outside their schools.

The 'green' jobhunter has a strong disadvantage compared to the weather-beaten, experienced jobhunter. It is an unfair battle.

Unemployed

When the labour market is less willing, it is (especially for starters) difficult to find a (suitable) job. That's why you can most certainly expect these important questions during the interview: 'How long have you been looking for work in vain?' 'What do you do with all your free time?'

What is a smart answer if you have spent a long time searching for a suitable job (in your community, the country, abroad) without any result?

- Make clear that (since graduation) you have been quite busy looking for a job that (somewhat) fits your training (and work experience). The future employer is probably aware of the labour market situation.
- Tell that you are not applying for every job opening that comes your way, but are only applying within one cluster of positions.
- Explain that careful jobhunting is also work, and requires a lot of time.
- Make it known that you support yourself by occasionally doing temp work.
- Convince them that in order to gain more experience in the field, or to not fall behind, you have taken on a part-time internship or that you are involved in the industry association, student organisation, user's platform, etc. Besides, you read the trade journals every month, visit trade fairs and congresses and take part in other professional activities and events.
- Share that you are following course X in order to gain more understanding and expertise.

By mentioning one or more of these points, you show that you are active, energetic and take initiative.

Applying for a job outside your field of study

In the past, when life was still simple, the choice of study pretty well always determined one's profession. Nowadays, most graduates end up in a position that is remotely related to their education – or entirely outside it. Even if one originally works in one's own profession, many choose a different path over time.

When you do not want anything to do with your diploma or there are no (suitable) jobs, then expect a flood of questions about your original choice and why you are now looking elsewhere for work. Why did you study sociology, while you now want to market a magazine? Why did you study physics, while you now are interested working for a venture capitalist doing financial analyses? Why did you take a personnel management course, while you now want to enter the field of export marketing? The interviewer will not be surprised by a significant switch – he or she is used to that.

The fact that there are no jobs that fit your chosen field is a plausible motivation for trying something else. No-one will blame you for taking that kind of initiative. But that is not the definitive answer. You have to show *why* you have chosen this particular sector or profession (position). The question remains: are you, despite your training, made of the right stuff?

While answering that question, use the opportunity to clearly spell out what you have learned during your school years and what (despite the great differences) can directly or indirectly be applied to the position you are aiming at. Perhaps the only thing is that you have become an excellent *analytical thinker*. That is tremendous, since that skill can be applied everywhere.

The uphill battle against experienced competitors

One often-heard complaint of new entrants to the labour market is that they by definition have no work experience, which they run up against time and time again. This way they will never get a suitable position. How do you fight back in a battle that already seems to be lost? How to compensate for this (temporary) shortcoming? A few tips to diminish the gap between you and the experienced competitor:

- You have no practical experience in this position, because that is impossible. But you do possess comparable work experience from summer jobs, jobs within the family business, tutoring and the like.
- Even though a lot of little jobs do not make a career, you have still gained a large repertoire of general knowledge working at temporary jobs and other functions you have had.
- The completed internship(s) and graduation paper(s) are valuable discussion points, especially when these relate to the organisation and/or the desired position.
- Explain that you learn quickly and pick things up fast.
- Argue for the chance to follow internal and external courses (if necessary, pay part or all of the costs –within reason, of course).
- Suggest that the employer assign a mentor or internal supervisor to you.
- Being assigned an external coach, especially during the tricky first period, may be valuable. The costs for the boss are probably nothing compared to the much higher salary that experienced candidates are asking.

Lowering the risks

Money is the blood flowing through the veins of every organisation. How can you overcome your handicap? By doing 'something with money'? More precisely: by transferring the risk from the employer to yourself. For example, offer to work for a certain period of time (one or two months) for free, or accept half the salary – which will be compensated in the future. Maybe an ultra-short labour contract (for example three months) will help to convince the employer.

Summary

Main points

1. Make sure you leave an impression in the interview, that you 'stick'. This includes posing sharp and critical questions.
2. Look for usable personal information about your future discussion partner(s) and the company. Research is the key word.
3. Add some fire (enthusiasm and passion) to the interview.
4. Practice giving analytical answers, whereby you unravel a definition or job vacancy to its core elements.
5. As a starter, your biggest problem will be lack of work experience. Think of how you can minimise that gap between the experience the employer wants and your current situation. Point out how the risk of joining the company can be shifted.

Worthwhile websites

Lge.gov.uk	About age discrimination
Learn.geek/interview.com	Tips for (almost) graduates
Sentient-recruitment.com	Info about the STAR-method
192.com	Finding people

With the help of the following chapter you will get closer to that desired job, if you can find a way to cross the interview and assessment river dry and intact.

7

CARRY OUT:

INTERVIEWS AND ASSESSMENTS

In the previous chapter you prepared yourself for the job interview. Now it is time to broadcast the right pieces at the right time 'live'. It is tough: during the interview, there is nowhere to hide, not behind a boss, colleagues, the trade union or government ministers.

The employer wants to avoid hiring the wrong candidate, but similarly, you don't want to discover after two days at your new job that it is nothing like you had imagined or was described to you. Therefore, everything must be carefully investigated during the interview and assessment, if the parties are meant for each other. In this chapter we are going to look at what you have to produce in the assessment, as far as the psychological test or assessment centre are concerned.

It is important to remember: it is not always the best candidate who gets the job, but the good candidate that is the most convincing during the selection procedure. In the C-phase (Carry out) you will have to perform, be careful and alert. More than ever, you cannot permit casualness or tomfoolery.

Beating a dead horse

During times of personnel shortages, employers, in their unbounded optimism, want to beat, smack and push on an almost any dead horse. Not any more for the time being: no-one will pull on you and beg and pray that you please join the employer's team. More importantly, companies are looking for that **perfect fit** with the top candidate. You are easily under or overqualified, too old, too young, too this, too that. You cannot strike a deal because you just don't fit, since you have not worked for a direct competitor or because you cannot be productive from off day one.

You will now have to work and race (around) like a horse. If the interviewer falls asleep during your meeting, then *you* have a problem. (Maybe he does too – but that is an entirely different matter.)

Fear!

Most jobhunters are a bit scared, uncertain, shy or nervous of their 'appearance' in a job interview or assessment. What are people afraid of? Some are afraid of standing in the spotlight (if they are not used to it). Others are afraid that all kinds of painful questions will be asked, that the interviewers will want to know everything, and invade their privacy. Many are nervous about the assessment tests and simulations. There may also be a fear of 'authority' or of people who have your fate in their hands, who can make or break your future.

Fear is a poor fellow traveller. Instead, be assertive: defend your own interest and don't let yourself be defeated. This interview may be very important, but if you are not selected, then you will no doubt get the chance to 'do it again', somewhere else. Failing is not the end of the world – and if it is, then your worries are over for good...

The interview

While you can quietly compose your letter and CV at home in your own time, during the interview there is a time limit. You will have a maximum of one hour to shine and show who you are, what abilities you have and why the choice should fall on you. During the interview you can only rely on yourself. If you mess it up, it's over. By preparing skilfully, you will make sure that your words don't evaporate like dust in the wind.

Orientation or job interview?

In theory, there are big differences between an orientation interview and a job interview. In the former, neither party has any obligations; in the latter, there is an implicit agreement that further steps will be taken if the candidate is suitable.

Job interview: the candidate...	Orientation interview: the candidate...
Sells himself	Can speak frankly
Has to be very knowledgeable about the employer	Can ask a lot of questions out of interest
Is protected by the employer's code of ethics	Is not protected by a code of ethics
Can be formally rejected	May tell that the job is not what expected
Travel and lodging expenses will be reimbursed, if that is standard practice at this employer's	All expenses are carried by oneself

What is the explicit goal of your interview: orientation or job? And is that your idea as well as the employer's?

'Why' questions?

Expect a lot of questions that begin with 'why'. These focus on your motivation, capabilities and talents, the kind of work you have done and the results of your efforts.

Asking 'why' questions is easy for the selection specialist, but you can work yourself into a corner with them, because you are forced to think about the underlying reasons and at the same time answer convincingly. You cannot just venture an opinion like in everyday life and leave it at that.

!!!! DANGER !!!!

Be careful that you don't blurt out any company secrets. The opponent will be thankful and may make good use of this information, but you will be punished for being indiscrete. So you will lose twice...

Language use

Old fashioned and taboo words

When you are older and still want to come across as (relatively) young and dynamic, you may want to pay special attention to your language. We don't mean that you have to throw in the latest, hippest, most fashionable words, but be careful about sentences that give away your age.

- *At my age...*
- *When I started working...*
- *Back then...*
- *When I was younger...*
- *It was during the best part of my life*
- *Before, I was good at...*
- *I remember it like it just happened yesterday...*
- *When you have reached my age...*
- *People my age...*
- *In the (good) old days..*

And then there are words that can get you into trouble:

- *fight (with my boss)*
- *(potential) conflict*

- *dishonesty*
- *hidden agendas*
- *political game (political animals)*
- *frustration*
- *tension*
- *no team player*
- *cheating, deceiving, swindling*

Words that do sell

During the job interview you have to convince the other person. Use powerful words like:

- *accurate*
- *active*
- *adjustable*
- *alert*
- *assertive*
- *brave*
- *businesslike*
- *calm*
- *capable*
- *careful*
- *competent*
- *competitive*
- *confident*
- *cooperative*
- *creative*
- *decisive*
- *democratic*
- *efficient*
- *emotionally intelligent*

- *energetic*
- *enthusiastic*
- *entrepreneurial*
- *extraverted*
- *flexible*
- *good humoured*
- *hardworking*
- *helpful*
- *humorous*
- *independent*
- *inventive*
- *loyal*
- *open*
- *optimistic*
- *organised*
- *patient*
- *persevering*
- *persistent*
- *powerful*

- *practical*
- *progressive*
- *quick*
- *rational*
- *realistic*
- *reasonable*
- *relaxed*
- *responsible*
- *sensitive*
- *stable*
- *strategic*
- *strong*
- *systematic*
- *tolerant*
- *trustworthy*
- *trustworthy*
- *understanding*
- *versatile*
- *warm*

Web interview

When we talk about interviews, we basically point at the personal, face to face meeting. But technically speaking, that can also occur digitally, for instance via Skype, MSN or a professional system. Considering the expected cost savings, these methods should do very well, in any case as a pre-selection method. The advantages will be chiefly in spanning long distances such as international job applications.

TIP

Is there just one day, or less, to go before the job interview? Go on line to check the most recent information and any relevant news about the company you are about to visit. A rise in the world sugar price by one cent may not mean much to you, but for the soft drink factory that you want to join, that penny will swallow up a considerable amount of their profit. When you spread around (this kind of) news, it shows that you are truly motivated to get this job, since you have insight in the organisation's activities.

The pillars of a 'standard interview'

A common interview model looks something like this, chronologically:

- *Mutual personal introduction*: exchange of polite greetings, the offered drinks ritual; the job applicant with his knocking knees and sweating underarms is put at ease.
- *Information* about the organisation, its goals, history, any future plans, tasks and responsibilities of the job etc.
- *Questions* asked about the CV and the candidate's ambition and clarification of unclear items.
- The job applicant can now *ask questions* to the interviewer (informative and procedural).

- *Saying goodbye,* with the promise of a follow-up (acceptance, rejection, next meeting).

What do most interviewers (employers, P&O managers, recruiters, etc) want to know from you? Almost everything! Sometimes they will dig to the very bottom. The following topics are always en vogue:

- *Personality*: Who are you? Are there any red flags? (Peculiarities, abnormalities, sickliness, stability and ability to deal with stress?)
- *Capabilities*: What do you know and what can you do? What are your competencies and talents? How well do you get along with people? (How good are your social skills?) Do you have leadership qualities?
- *Motivation*: What do you want? Are you driven? Why exactly do you fancy working for us, in this position? How involved (connected) are you in your community, in society at large? How *deep* does your motivation go? The interested interviewer determines this by firing questions at you like: 'Which trade journals do you know?' Or even sharper: 'Have you read the latest issue of the trade magazine XYZ? And what impressed you most?' Don't be at a loss of words.
- *Cultural match*: Do you fit in? Can you adjust to us – and do you want to? Are you OKP (Our Kind of People)? This is probably the most difficult part for both parties. That's why it is smart to gather the necessary information by reading and talking to people who know this organisation (preferable through and through).
- *Potential*: What do you have (even more) to offer on behalf of our mutual future? Leadership capabilities?
- *Ambition*: What are your future plans? How do they fit into the employer's? (Present yourself as an 'investor' instead of a member of the audience!)

Types of questions

Interviewers have a wide range of questions at their disposal:

- *Open and closed questions.* An open question is for example: 'Why do you prefer A?' You are freer to talk with open questions. Keep to concrete behaviour as much as possible. A closed question is: 'Do you prefer A or B?'
- *Cross examination.* A well-seasoned interviewer will always use cross examination. 'Can you give an example of this?' 'Please go into more detail.' 'How did you specifically do that then?' A good piece of advice: illustrate your stories with *facts* and *examples*.
- *Repetitive questions.* If you answer a question unsatisfactorily at the beginning of the interview, the interviewer may repeat the question later on. The danger is that you don't remember what you had said before and so will come up with something else.
- *Trick questions.* If the interviewer thinks that you are holding back essential information or are lying, then he will go fishing – or hunting. You say that you have been working for some time as a freelancer. If he does not trust that, then later on, there will be a question about how much you earned during that period. Or: 'First you said A and now you say B. What is the story?'
- *Reflective questions.* To check if you can reflect on something – and how you do it. 'What do you find difficult about this question?'
- *Hypothetical questions.* 'Imagine, you are a management trainee and it is your first workday... What would you do?'
- *Self-liquidating questions.* Those questions that you do *not* want to answer! E.g. 'What is the biggest mistake that you have ever made (at work)?'
- *Wide-open questions.* Many candidates have difficulty with broadly posed questions which can go off in any direction and which they have not thought about before, like:

- 'What is your vision of life?' (You are almost being asked about your vision of the universe.)
- 'What are all your aspirations?'
- 'Which general values and principles are dear to you?'
- 'What do you bring to the table, if hired for this position?'

Everyone has a (life's) story to tell, but limit your answer to crucial points. Elaboration is not done, because then you apparently cannot separate the major issues from the secondary ones.

TIP

A rule of thumb: if you don't understand a question, ask for clarification – but don't do that too often.

The infamous 'first minute' and the undervalued 'last minute'

The first impression that you make is extremely important. That does not apply so much with top interviewers, but for their colleagues who don't interviews daily. Their verdict has been made, even before one word has been spoken. The candidate, with the droopy shoulders and bowed head, without any eye contact, who shuffles into the 'examination room' without a word, with folded arms and completely rigid (or even worse, who stays standing), will find it difficult to shake off the impression that he is uncertain. It is better to walk into the room proud and upright, while offering your hand and a big smile, and to give your full attention right away to the potential opponent.

However, the *last minute* is also important. Do not let it peter out. Keep the conversation lively, ask questions and continue showing your optimism. If you don't believe in yourself anymore, will the other person do? What do you think? Do not weaken, be aware of the impression you are making (non-verbal communication), until you have left the room and are out of sight.

Reasons for leaving: the six p's

It is quite logical that an interviewer asks why you are looking for a job or why you want to leave your present employer. 'Due to an involuntary dismissal' may be the honest answer, but it is not always wise to report that. What can you say? Keep the six p's in mind:

1. **P**romotion possibilities: there is no opportunity to grow within the company (within the short term).
2. **P**rickles, challenges: the stimulus has disappeared. You have seen it all, done it all.
3. **P**lace: the long commute (traffic jams) is unbearable.
4. **P**ounds: you are not happy (anymore) with your salary and rewards, or you have reached the top end of the scale.
5. **P**restige: you have decided to work for a more reputable employer, a company with a solid name.
6. **P**roblems with finance: the current employer is heading towards bankruptcy or your job may become redundant due to an imminent reorganisation or merger. You want to be one step ahead.

A negative motivation is no option. Don't allow yourself to say something like:

- 'A friend told me about this vacancy.'
- 'I was fired; that is why I am looking for a (another) job.'
- 'Well, you know, every oil company is the same.'
- 'I cannot get along with my boss at all.'

Save what can be saved

It can be that at a certain moment during the job interview, you feel or even know that the battle is finished and you have lost. Then what? There is a minimal chance that it can still be won by doing something surprising, daring or unorthodox. You must push the discussion into a different direction. Take the chance, as your lot is hanging from a silk thread anyway.

TIP

Turn what seems to be a disadvantage into an advantage. Your ingredients? Creativity, courage, quick thinking and a bit of optimism.

It is also *your* interview: be a *partner*

You can answer all the questions that are fired at you politely and submissively. There is nothing against that. But if you want to present yourself as a true interview partner, then you will have to dare to introduce topics yourself, ask questions, touch upon emotions and steer the conversation.

It is necessary that you hold the other person's attention. If you lose it (the other nods vaguely, looks at his watch or outside, suppresses a yawn, lets you babble on), then your words will just evaporate. You will control the interview by not only listening carefully, but also by paying attention to the interviewer's expected non-verbal s signals (or the lack of these). If the other person is not paying attention, it is time to change your tactic.

Descriptive answers

If an interviewer reports that he has not gotten to know you (a firm model statement from the *'Great Interviewers' Handbook'*), then you have probably used too many descriptive answers. These could be correct, but you are not showing your true colours, the answers do not reveal your 'soul'. What they are looking for are **'interpretative'** answers. An example: your reply to the question, why you would like to work for Air France/KLM, refers to the number of airplanes that this French-Dutch consortium owns – and that can be entirely true. But it does not say anything about what 'moves' you. That's why you should 'translate' a message for your listener once in a while: 'For me, that *means* that I...'

TIP

It is one thing to say that you are (have been) *effective* at your job. That means that the intended results have always been achieved. It is another thing to say that you kept within a time limit or a budget, in other words were *efficient* (or *productive*).

Twenty short and powerful tips
Accept the following advice from the jobhunting whisperer:

1. Always be on time – preferably be early. 'I was in a traffic jam' is a poor excuse, the same goes for 'I missed the bus' or 'the drawbridge was open'. What does that say about someone? At the very least it will cost you your interview time. Take a test ride ahead of time. You will feel more sure and relaxed.
2. Stick a diary with you to set down or check new appointments and a notebook to make notes. Think about appropriate clothing and accessories.
3. Let the interviewer take the lead. Don't correct his mistakes (loss of face!), except with regards to your CV.
4. Speak the employer's jargon and language, for example in terms of turnover, profit, image or service.
5. However paradoxical, you have come to talk, but careful *listening* and *observing* are of utmost importance. You should not babble on without stopping. Keep calm, relaxed and alert!

6. Use positive words. Don't start a debate; try not to win an argument.
7. *Avoid problem areas.* Do not bring up issues that will reflect badly on you or that distract you from the main point. Do not talk about your pet topic. That is not why you are there.
8. Don't complain (about your current or former employer, the sector, your life, the weather).
9. Ask relevant questions about the organisation and the position. Keep reminding yourself that it is also *your* interview.
10. Be friendly but not too familiar. Do not use first names. Do not act as if you have known the interviewer(s) for years.
11. Don't rush or interrupt the other persons – even if they are going on and on.
12. Sell what you know (your knowledge and skills), not who you know. (Don't try to impress the selection agent by name dropping.)
13. Think first before you react to a difficult question. Wishy-washy answers will not be rewarded.
14. Keep eye contact at all times (no prying eyes!) and pay attention to your posture (and your interviewer's).
15. Don't talk about financial matters yet. Keep that for the last meeting.
16. *Do not beat around the bush* if you really don't have the answer. You are not supposed to know everything! (As long as you *can* give a suitable answer to most of the questions.)
17. Sell yourself based on your track record, the results you have achieved at the latest employer(s). That is the business card you leave behind. Offer concrete facts, figures and examples.
18. People often shoot themselves in the foot by downplaying, weakening or emphasising the negative points of their own achievements. Be thrifty using the word 'but' (which often means 'no').

19. Present you arguments in order of importance. That is because a sharp, experienced interviewer will pay attention to that.
20. Make notes *after* the interview. For example, about which questions you found difficult, so that you can improve your next presentation.

Every rejection is a chance!

Many selection specialists have difficulty looking candidates deep into the eyes and rejecting them right away. Giving the message in writing or digitally is less painful for both parties, since it is in the privacy of one's home. Find out after *each* rejection why you were not chosen. Make it your SOP (*Standard Operating Procedure*). Build up your courage: every day holds the promise of new opportunities!

Assessments and psychological tests

The standard psychological procedure most often tests qualities like intelligence, personality, management capabilities and styles and others (for example attention and concentration, accuracy and administrative skills). The interview with the psychologist in always part of the 'examination'. (And equally important as any test.)

Intelligence tests

In almost every selection test, the test giver wants to know how the candidate scores compared to the norm, a large group of people with the same educational background, age and other properties. Unfortunately, there are two problems. (Not counting that we barely know what the construct of intelligence is, but that is just a detail... There is an abundance of theories on this intriguing subject.) Firstly, the candidates from a homogenous group (for instance civil engineers) will supposedly not vary much from each other. So what is the point in assessing their IQ? Secondly, that being the case, what does that actually mean for the execution and quality of the professional's work? For example, is the engineer with a lower IQ by definition less skilled? And how can you actually verify that?

Nevertheless, the future employer will still want to know more about your intelligence. This is based on the theory that the higher the IQ, the more abstract and conceptual your thinking and the faster and easier you learn compared to others. Some people believe that IQ is the best predictor of success at work. One good reason for intelligence testing is that diploma-inflation has resulted in uncertainty about the value of certain master degrees. What is the worth of the title Master of Rubber Boots (Mrb) from the University of Shittytown? This test is useful when candidates have to have a bachelor's degree (minimal requirement), but what if a very experienced and otherwise qualified candidate without this degree applies? How to deal with that? A test will verify her level.

A whole battery of tests are usually administered. Every subtest investigates one facet of intelligence. The most popular ones are analogies, synonyms, verbal-critical reasoning, number series, calculus, numerical critical reasoning (interpretation of tables and figures), dynamic and static figures.

TIP

For examples, practice and the tricks of the trade, we refer you to *All about Psychological Tests and Assessment Centres* and *The IQ-Trainer*.

Personality tests

Personality tests are questionnaires that systematically reveal a number of facets (but not all) of one's character, such as independence, rigidity and dominance, to name a few. There are many of these tests, which all measure different characteristics or traits. There is no standard format or terminology, but it looks like standardisation in testland will occur, in the form of the 'Big Five'.

These are the following five personality traits that are often measured:

- neuroticism (emotional instability);
- extraversion (energy and attention directed to the outside world);
- openness (curiosity for the internal and the external world);
- altruism (helping the weak);
- conscientiousness (accuracy, moral sense and reliability).

Every question relates to a certain characteristic. It is difficult to figure out which characteristic is related to each question, if you are not familiar with the subject matter. Do not concentrate blindly on the literal wording of the questions themselves: it has to do with what each item measures, what its contribution is to the trait to which it belongs. While you are filling in the questionnaire keep one thing in mind: what will the profile of the 'ideal candidate' look like? Answer accordingly.

Management tests

Management tests determine if someone is suitable for a (future) supervisory or management position. The assignments vary from written personality-type of inventories, commercial tests, and arranging mini trains on a model railway, to solving theoretical or practical management or marketing case studies.

While the open assignments differ per test agency and they are not really a test (they have not been standardised), there are still a number of points to consider. Firstly, you have to keep in mind that during a practical exercise you may be observed. Demonstrate that you approach problems *creatively*, *logically*, *analytically* and *systematically* (do not shoot widely in every direction), while speed is less important. Ask yourself the following questions:

- What exactly is the problem?
- Which factors play a role here? (social, task-oriented, commercial)
- What things are connected?

- Which problems need to be addressed first? (internal/external)
- What are the consequences for choosing this approach?

E-tests

Electronically administered tests are enjoying an increased popularity. More and more consultancy agencies offer the possibility to take intelligence and personality tests from the comfort of your own home (or a clever friend's) via the internet. The security for such a test consists of a password that you receive ahead of time. The content of these tests is not any different from their original paper versions; only the way you take the tests is different. For example with a paper version you can make notes, while that is more difficult or impossible on the screen (in a controlled situation).

The assessment centre

An assessment centre (AC) is an extensive practical simulation ('work sample test'), consisting of a number of (mostly standard) behavioural exercises. The behaviour of the candidate is observed by one or more assessors (observers/testers), based on a limited number of predetermined behavioural dimensions. The goal is to determine if someone's qualities and capabilities are sufficient to successfully carry out the job. In other words, *behaviour predicts behaviour*, since the testee is dealing with concrete situations. There are unique ACs which have been developed for just one organisation. But usually standard methods are applied, which at the very most, are adjusted to some of the client's wishes (customisation). The AC is most often applied by (psychological) selection agencies, but some big employers (multinationals for instance) also make use of them.

Just to be clear: assessment centres don't have anything to do with centres of some kind. 'Centre' means that the candidate is put in a central position (to be studied). The AC is based on job relevant and observable behaviours, like leadership, persuasion and flexibility. The method is transparent for both parties: the candidate executes tasks that are somewhat related to his own (or future) work.

Since the AC has gotten a less favourable reputation here and there, some selection bureaus and organisations also euphemistically call it a development centre nowadays. It sounds better that only the weak points are mapped out, so that you can improve yourself (via training and schooling). However, the end result remains the same: you are rejected because there is too much you have to 'work on'...

Measuring potential

Job applicants are also tested for their future qualities and ambitions. Some airlines select their future pilots not only based on their flying skills (what a relief!) but also on the *potential* to become a captain. They must be able to demonstrate their leadership abilities. Is it expected that you grow in the new job? Or is it going to be your final destination? Do your utmost during these tests, even for parts which you think have nothing to do with carrying out the position competently.

AC exercises

In the assessment centre you carry out a variety of simulations. That could be just two (big ones), or a series of smaller ones. There are group and individual assignments. For example, a typical group assignment is a discussion – and that is not just shooting the breeze, as you may have thought. A short overview of the most important assignments:

- *In-tray.* One of the best-known exercises is dealing with internal and external post. What is being assessed here? Your skills in the areas of planning and organisation, delegating, management control, judgment, decision-making, problem analysis, setting priorities, taking initiative, written communication, organisational sensitivity, independence.

- *Role play*. Another popular type is the role play, between a manager and an employee, a salesperson and a client etc. This is not surprising since good verbal communication is essential on the work floor. For instance the test determines if you are result-driven or can motivate others.
- *Fact-finding*. You must first draw conclusions based on somewhat vague facts that you have managed to obtain and after that you present your recommendations. The sharper your questions during the 'cross-examination', the better the information you will get. How will you approach this situation? Which plan or structure will you execute? Is the unfolding story logical? Are you offering one or more solutions? Which one do you endorse? Do you dare to stick your neck out? Or do you ultimately allow the other person to choose? Don't!
- *Bad news talk*. During this role play you (the testee) first receive the necessary information about a department or an employee. After some (often limited) preparation you have to give this worker the bad news, such as telling that he is going to be fired, transferred or will get a pay cut. How do you do this effectively, while staying in charge?
- *Analysis and presentation*. You have to first analyse a certain amount of information (often limited, or which you must expand on). Then you have to clarify your vision of the problem and the solution or plan (marketing plan, investment alternative), based on the information. Finally, you have to present this, for instance to a few 'board members' (assessors). What will you base your final decision on? Tell them!
- *Group discussion*. After having carried out preparatory work, you will get into a discussion with several other candidates or agency recruits about a business problem. During the entire meeting your behaviour will be carefully observed and judged. You will have to continually be at your best! These discussions are often *leaderless* (no leader assigned). However, the expectation is that the 'natural' leader will

emerge. (You?) Well-known group assignments include: determining the budget, whereby the candidates have to make a compromise, or selection of a promotable employee. In a *meeting simulation* you have to play the chairperson or a regular member. This is a valued exercise, if meetings threaten to become an important part of your new position.

* *Writing reports.* Job applicants for policy advisory positions can expect a (re)writing assignment. After analysing and interpreting the written material (reports, financial overviews and the like), you get to work. Some information is unclear, unnecessary or ambiguous, and at times badly needed information is left out on purpose.

Once in a while candidates are confronted with **integral** assessments. That means for instance that the in-tray and role play are based on the same information. An in-tray document indicates that you have to quickly do a performance review with employee Ellerts. At the **dynamic** in-tray, while you are working zealously, your concentration is broken by a ringing phone on your desk or by an 'employee' who forces a new report under your nose which you have to read right away.

TIP

Use your imagination and break out of the exercises' limitations, within reason, if it will make life easier for you.

Behavioural dimensions, meta dimensions and competencies

The candidate's behaviour is judged on so-called behavioural dimensions, whereby usually, A 1 is poor and a 5 excellent. Below, you will find a number of common dimensions, divided down into five categories, each with two examples:

1. *Individual behaviour*
   - *Decisiveness*: is able to (quickly) make decisions resulting in a judgement and/or action; considers the consequences in the short and long term; can defend his/her decisions.
   - *Creativity*: is able to come up with original solutions for problems related to the position; knows how to think up a new approach for replacing existing methods and techniques; is innovative.

2. *Interpersonal (relationship) behaviour*
   - *Assertiveness*: is powerful dealing with others; can take the lead (if necessary); is decisive and dares to take risks – even if the decision is based on limited information.
   - *Leadership*: can give direction and steering to a group and stimulates cooperation uses the correct style to reach the group's goals; monitors and evaluates progress; shows vision and inspiration; develops skills and competencies with his workers and motivates them.

3. *Management behaviour*
   - *Organisational insight*: Is able to grasp internal problems and possibilities and take action; in doing so, considers the consequences for all stakeholders (employees, clients, suppliers and the like).
   - *Delegating*: can correctly divide tasks and activities, decision-making authority and responsibilities amongst employees, puts them to work effectively; pays attention to the level where the decision can be made; monitors the procedures and regulates the processes.

4. *Motivational behaviour*
   - *Initiative*: is able to notice chances and acts on them; prefers to initiate and influence situations rather than waiting passively.
   - *Performance motivation*: sets high standards for his/her own work and those of others, is not satisfied with an average performance; makes complete use of available

time and resources; finishes a task, despite various barriers that arise; can manage himself/herself.

5. *Intellectual behaviour*
   - *Analytical ability*: Is able to identify problems and collect relevant information; can process numerical information (financial, statistical) accurately and draw meaningful interpretations; can make decisions based on logical assumptions that reflect factual information.
   - *Critical thinking*: has the ability to reason logically, draw realistic conclusions from facts, recognise assumptions, differentiate between strong and weak arguments.

Sometimes a **broader division** is used, such as in five meta dimensions or 'powers':

1. *Thinking power* (thinking) – examples: logical thinking, creativity, organisational sensitivity.
2. *Social power* (feeling) – examples: listening, empathy, persuasion.
3. *Action power* (doing) – examples: management abilities, management control, and an eye for costs/benefits.
4. *Will power* (wanting) – examples: taking initiative, perseverance, energy.
5. *Balance* (the balance between the four powers) – examples: personal insight, maturity, self-control.

Another way to divide this is by competencies, namely the combination of behaviour criteria. One selection agency describes the competency 'impact' as 'performance with dynamism and flair, makes and maintains contact easily, representative, makes a good impression due to results, presents ideas well, keeps his attention, can argue convincingly, has a natural authority. This competency consists of the behavioural criteria: verbal presentation, persuasiveness, performance and social skills'.

However, there are also other traits, behaviours and properties that may be reported:

- What is the candidate's memory like?
- Is he/she 'warm', sympathetic?
- Can he/she concentrate and pay attention to details?

Disqualifiers

In some ACs 'disqualifiers' are applied: behavioural criteria which the candidate must satisfactorily fulfil, or else... (for example at least a 3 on the 5 point scale). This score cannot be compensated, since the employer (or the selection agency) assumes this trait is crucial for performing the job competently, and less is not acceptable. An example of a disqualifier is 'persuasion', which an employer will deem as essential for the sought-after salesperson.

The psychological interview

Along with the cited tests and simulations, there will always be a talk with a psychologist, in which your past will be discussed, as well as the position. The interview is a second test situation for the psychologist, where he can compare your test profile (paper) with how you present yourself (life). Whether the interview or the (paper) tests are more important depends on the tester. In general, the psychologist wants to see a consistent picture. That means that the results from tests and the interview must correspond with each other, since the employer wants to make sure there are no 'hidden deficiencies'.

If you are interested in the code of conducts (ethics) of psychologists please visit www.bps.org.uk.

Reporter is adviser

The results from the entire assessment are compiled in a report. If you have a problem with this piece or with your selection psychologist, keep in mind that the report always contains an advice and the good man or woman is always an adviser. The client (employer) holds the key, and can follow the advice or reject it.

Psychological selection agencies

The websites of most psychological selection agencies are not very informative. You can read about their philosophy (not really interesting for a job applicant), and get to know their 'culture'. However, there are also agencies that treat you to an interactive pre-test. Be careful, in general their examples are considerably easier than their real tests.

Case study as surprise attack

It may happen that headhunters and recruitment and selection agencies, totally unannounced, will present you with a case study. You are then casually requested to make a short analysis, or present a recommendation. If you suspect this could be the case, refresh your knowledge of resolving case study assignments, so that you can keep your footing on D-day.

Summary

Main points

1. Interviewers are always looking for logic and reasons. Expect a lot of **why** questions.
2. In order to determine your suitability, interviewers look into these major categories: personality, capabilities, motivation, cultural match, potential and ambition.
3. The last minute of the interview is just as important as the infamous first minute.
4. Prepare yourself ahead of time for the possibility of taking psychological tests and assessment centre simulations.
5. The external selection agency's report contains advice, it is not the final judgement. The client makes the final decision. (So there may be some leeway if you are rejected by the agency.)

Worthwhile websites

Careers.ed.ac.uk	Assessment exercises and tests
Shl.com	Various practice tests
123tests.com	Self-tests (IQ, personality and the like)
Prospects.ac.uk	Various tests and assessment simulations
Bsp.org.uk	Behaviour code for British psychologists

If you have 'made it through', then comes the concluding step: the employment contract, possibly after the negotiation. This is the topic of the following and final chapter.

8

SIGN THE CONTRACT:

NEGOTIATING THE BEST SALARIES AND BENEFITS

After a turbulent journey across the jobhunting sea, a safe harbour has been spotted. Now you have to get that dough. You can accept the offer right away, which is sometimes wise. However, you may get a better deal or perhaps you don't want to work for the pittance being offered. Take plenty of time and be well prepared for the salary discussion, since this will put you in a much better starting position. Even if the employer's offer is firm and fixed – he hides himself behind a standard labour agreement – there are still many possibilities to jack up your total income. There is the chance you will meet a formidable opponent; at the very least it will be someone who has swung the axe a few more times than you.

For many, one of the most important aspects of a job is pleasure at work. Salary and future opportunities come secondary. Without fun, your motivation will shrink, which influences your performance – and you can draw your own conclusion... We will give you ideas to find your way out of a negotiation stalemate and to go on to plan B, in case you end up not being hired.

The reward for your hard work

Perhaps the job, which you are now fighting through the last details of, fulfils all your wishes. Perhaps you are less satisfied with the *conditions*, but what choice do you have during these hard times? Put some thought into it before you receive the well-intended congratulations from the Tax department as they start making deductions.

Imagine, the employer's offer initially makes you happy. Should you agree to it right away? Will you receive what you think you deserve every month in your bank account? However good his offer seems to be at first glance, there is often room for improvement, so it is often wise to not agree immediately. Ponder the offer carefully. Even if you gain a salary increase of only 1 percent, you are already ahead! And for many years to come.

Maybe you think that you have no power as a job applicant during these difficult times. But the employer is also at the end of his rope, at the end of a time-consuming and tiring procedure, and wants to cut a deal. He has already signalled that he is confident in you. You only need to put down your signature.

Benefits and salary negotiations

If you want to negotiate with the future boss (you don't have to!), keep the following in mind:

1. Your point of view is: this is not only about me. Rather, we both have to finish as winners.
2. You make it clear that you are interested in the long term: therefore, you want to be ever so careful and are spending the necessary time on the negotiation.
3. Do your homework. For example, investigate which remuneration is normal in this sector and for this kind of position. Or look at which possibilities the proposed employment contract (read it!) does offer. Which booty can you actually get a hold of?
4. What is important is the **total package** (gross salary *and* all the secondary benefits, taxable and un-taxable).
5. If you see yourself as a product or, preferably, a brand (a modern approach), then you will also dare to act like a marketeer and put yourself temporarily 'on sale', in other

words, lower your salary or accept a cut (if necessary). But maybe you are a premium brand...

6. Be creative and think along with the employer.
7. Consider the costs of a failed negotiation. Will you end up empty-handed?
8. Sometimes bosses are forgetful – which may be convenient for them... Make sure that at the end of the negotiation both parties have agreed to the *same* conditions. Check these, if the manager doesn't do so. (Ask for a verbal summary, followed by a written confirmation of the results of the negotiation.)
9. If you have not reached an agreement, don't repeat the now old and worn arguments. That is irritating and counter-productive; let those things ride. Your intermediate goal is to arrange a follow-up meeting. Perhaps you will succeed next time around.

Labour agreements and the like

It is easy for a boss to fall back on a standard labour agreement – and keep saying that 'everything is fixed'. But is that actually the case?

A standard contract is a starting point, not the destination – unless both parties are happy and satisfied with it. These are the steps to get out of a stalemate:

1. Suggest changing the job title. (You change one or two words! That's all...)
2. You go up a scale.
3. You also can negotiate on the timing and amount of the first raise, and the frequency of subsequent reviews. (You can 'play' around with this.)
4. Find out if clauses stipulating 'special rewards', or market-driven compensation are applicable to your situation.

Keep in mind at all times:

- your plea must be supported with strong arguments – put yourself in the role of a tough lawyer;
- the HR-manager is not paying you out of his own pocket;
- and that he wants to enlist a motivated and loyal employee – and that is worth something to him.

TIP

'Under-assistant to the personal assistant of the manager' (what a mouth full!) looks better on your business card than 'helping hand'. Which title do you prefer?

A practical point: salary components

What you will receive for your hard work, is not only a gross monthly salary. While that certainly is the most important part, there are many other elements, secondary benefits, which are also negotiable. We will name a few important ones:

- **Company car**. The company car is still one of the best known and loved secondary benefits. If you acquire one: are you allowed to assume ownership at a certain point in time (if you want)? Will it be offered to you at a predetermined and favourable price?
- **Expense account**. This is the monthly tax-free allowance in order to carry out your work properly, without the fuss and bothers of receipts. Perhaps that will be profitable for you?
- **Travel allowance**. This compensation is for commuting or business travel.
- **Telephone costs**. It is not incorrect to assume that you may make a lot of business calls at home and will use the internet for work. Bring the mobile phone and the personal digital assistant into the negotiation as well.

- **Collective insurance.** Many businesses have an arrangement with one or more insurance companies, which makes it possible for you to get attractive discounts on various premiums.
- **Company savings plans.** What does the organisation offer?
- **Pension.** An important and very complex component. Which part does the employer pay and which part the employee? Is this retirement package transferable to a new employer? Quite often it is worth to contact an external specialist.
- **Profit sharing.** Profit sharing/bonuses/thirteenth month. A financial reward based on the company's results and/or your performance.
- **Overtime.** In many companies, higher ranking employees are expected to work overtime without any compensation. But: if it is assumed that you will structurally be working 60 hours a week, then a 40 hour salary will clearly not be a fair compensation.
- **Flexible working hours.** This is convenient for employees with children or workers who would rather avoid those tiresome traffic jams.
- **Education.** Here are plenty of topics for discussion. You have understood that schooling is highly important during your career. Some organisations are very generous and have a special fund for educational needs. For others it is a necessity, due to the rapid changes in technology or regulations (for instance in ICT or accountancy). Try to set down an *individual* yearly budget for training and development. This can be combined with a 100 percent compensation for passing and 50 percent (or nothing) for failing the course. Also bring the accompanying costs into the negotiation, such as study books and materials, travel expenses and examination fees.
- **Conventions/study tours.** Is there a (personal) budget for these? How big is it? Will you be able to reach the Bahamas with it?
- **Holidays.** While the number of days is usually standard, there are also ways of getting more through negotiation. (Don't

forget to pay attention to the number of annual obligatory free days.)

- **Discounts** on company products or services. Both internal and external (tax) rules may apply when 'shopping at the boss's store'!
- **Home computer or laptop**. You may be able to acquire a computer via the company at very generous terms (or for nothing).
- **Day care**. What is the company willing to fork out for you?

Don't assume that the future employer will burst out in song and dance when you bring one or more of these aspects to the negotiation table, or that he will quickly agree with each and every one of them.

TIP

The above list is not exhaustive. In the *Ultimate Guide to Salary Negotiation* you will find many more components, each accompanied by a detailed explanation.

'There are tens more like you'

You can't dismiss the chance that the obliging employer listens to you attentively, even understands your intelligent, rightful, and financially-sound wishes, but does not want to budge an inch. He simply cannot allow himself to. There are many other suitable candidates knocking on the door, he has plenty of choice. He can dismiss your points with the following arguments, which you will have to counter:

- 'It is a bad time.' *Your reaction*: 'But you still want to offer someone a contract.'

- 'Our turnover is suffering.' *Your reaction*: 'I have read/heard that the company is still making quite a profit.' (It is not terrible everywhere.)
- 'We cannot offer you any more.' *Your reaction*: 'I can understand that fewer people must work harder than ever before.'

Homework is key here: the better you are prepared, the easier the negotiation will go and you can squash all the objections that are thrown at you.

Who pays what

In order to determine if you will receive a fair salary, you first have to assess what your financial wishes are. Secondly, you need to look for suitable comparisons. The free salary websites (like Monsterboard.co.uk) may provide up-to-date information. Be aware that these are indications, which could differ a great deal from reality and what you have in mind. (Besides these, there are paid websites only open to subscribers – big organisations.) You can also refer to governmental websites, which match job titles with annual salaries. The government, which values openness so much (which naturally does not apply to politicians), allows you make use of its pay and rewards schemes.

At time both employees and employers experience the same problem: they are both unsure where the employee will end up in the future. Is the amount of the agreed on salary fair and just? Is it in accordance with the market place?

Don't rob the boss, but negotiate with principles

What do you do if you are both miles apart? Is a compromise still realistic? First, an explanation of negotiation which is not based on principles: just yelling anything out (a high amount) or meeting half way. That is not the way to go. What you do is point out past performance, which you describe in concrete and objective terms –

for example, realised turnover, acquired sponsorships, completed cost savings programmes, number of satisfied clients (shown by research), number of complaints (decreased), launched ideas (show an article from the company's in-house magazine).

In an ideal world the desired salary and everything associated with it is based on the fact that the HR-manager, or whoever your negotiation partner is, knows what you are worth. And so you will earn what you deserve...

Imagine that the other person suggests a 'price' that is 10 percent under your *realistic* (researched and justified) objective and does not want to alter it. What to do? As a principled negotiator you agree to this, but bring to the table that you will also work 10 percent less (half a working day). You abide by your principles, and the justification that goes along with it.

With the Tax Department's heartfelt compliments

Every animal has a natural enemy. For people, this is the Taxmen. Therefore, it is good to examine its Achilles heel, within the legal boundaries. Add up what is deducted from the salary and what is picked off from holiday pay, bonuses and other special rewards: a lot. You will easily be working for the first half of the year for the Tax Department – and then you start to earn for yourself. It is thus wise to make these calculations before you appear at the negotiation table. You can limit it here and there by shifting taxable remuneration to non-taxable remuneration. But be careful of future consequences (holiday pay, social benefits).

Employment contracts

The employment contract is an instrument which both parties want to refer to when later on opinions differ about certain items, memories fail or the employer and employee no longer feel comfortable with each other. Put time and energy into the contract you are offered, as a precaution. You want to play the devil's advocate in this stage.

Many employers make use of standard employment contracts – **their** standard. Some are favourable for the employee, most are obviously not. Keep in mind that you are *always* free to negotiate one or more clauses. That will prevent differences of opinion and nasty situations later on. Contracts can also be broken up at any time – ask any pro football player – but it takes two to tango.

Some employers offer their personnel a so-called benefits statement plan. This document spells out all the agreed financial benefits and entitlements, and what their gross and net values are.

TIP

Insist on having at least two performance reviews per year. Remain informed and alert.

Outplacement

While no-one starts a job with the idea of being involuntarily fired, employees (sometimes in droves) do sometimes get made redundant. This can be based on poor performance, a conflict, incompatibility, economic downturn and many other reasons. Long before the axe falls, you can build up a fortification against the onslaught. To begin with you can get legal aid insurance, for the incredibly high legal costs (the premiums are low) that you may incur in the future if you want to dispute a redundancy.

However, the insurance does not typically cover the costs of outplacement, whereby you receive professional help in seeking a new position. Our advice: discuss the possible costs with the employer and put your wishes down in writing. Placing this clause in your contract will not cost the employer any money, unless you get shown the door. This kind of clause will support you in case you are thrown out, especially during turbulent times and with high risk jobs. So be 'pessimistic' about the future when it comes to your employment contract.

Non-competition clause

The non-competition clause is a restriction in the employment contract. For instance, the employer obliges you, for a set period (often one year) after leaving, not to undertake any work in the same sector, either as an employee or working for yourself. Any violation is met with a forceful fine. Read the small print before you sign on the dotted line. Also this item of the contract, or parts of it, can be negotiated.

Sell yourself with flexibility

We have assumed that you want to get a permanent contract. Perhaps you will increase your chances with a willing employer by pointing out alternatives, in order to be on the same page.

You completely agree with the (future) employer that the company must stay flexible. Luckily there are all kinds of employment contracts, all of which have their pro's and con's, also in less flourishing times. For instance, you can have a temporary contract for a set period, not a standard year, but for three or six months or two or three years. If there is a glitch in the cable, then your contract will be ended, whether you are physically there or not. You may consider putting in a compensation clause if you are kicked out at a much early stage.

You can also offer to sign a project contract, for variable working hours, freelance (with or without 'guaranteed hours') or on-call basis. How flexible do you want to be? What do you prefer -and why that?

Flexi-work contract

A flexi-work contract offers you some protection from the bleak polar winds. Such an agreement is based on mutual understanding, openness and honesty. It sounds nice. Flexi-workers have some advantages compared to permanent employees:

- They are independent (and can also refuse assignments);

- They often earn more per job or period than colleagues with permanent positions;
- They have more and longer vacations (or none at all!);
- They choose their own development.

Flexi-workers are forced to consider their employment conditions more closely and more often than colleagues who enjoy a permanent contract. Points to worry about: trial period, holiday rights, changes in salary, termination of contract, lengthening of the contract, interim terminations, sick pay, overtime, parental leave, social benefits and pension.

Making conditional agreements
You could be so close to the job, but still have not signed the employment contract. The future employer wants to pay you less than what you whispered in his ear. Before you throw the towel into the ring, think of a *compromise*, at least if you both want to approach each other. Propose a conditional agreement. Some examples:

- If the company results in the coming period increase by x percent, your salary goes up as well: by y percent.
- If a company car becomes available within the next half year (you know that current employees will leave), then you are the first person in line to take over a car.
- You accept the manager's offer, with the condition that in six months your salary is increased by 5 percent and in twelve months again by a further 5 percent. (So that you ultimately reach your goal, although with a delay.)
- You propose to look for solutions that are financially attractive for both you and the employer. That means that the costs go down for the employer and the net amount for yourself remains about the same. For example, you make an (extra) pension fund contribution, you acquire the right to be schooled for so much money per year (sometimes a trade

association may support this as well) or to visit conventions and seminars (nice trips), you receive a clothing allowance or are allowed to take part in a deferred salary plan.

Plan B – if it does not work out

Imagine that all your efforts don't result in the desired job. On the one hand you have come across very few suitable vacancies, on the other hand you were shot down in the few interviews you did have. Now what?

Sooner or later it is wise to move on to plan B. Sooner, if you have not been able to find any jobs, because that means that you have a number of alternatives in mind. That will reduce your stress. Later, if there is nothing better on the horizon. What are the possibilities?

Job portfolio

Plan B could be a portfolio, a combination of two or three part-time jobs. (Of which one you would like to have as a full-time job.) All kinds of combinations are feasible, like teaching part-time at college (permanent income!) and working part-time as a coach. Or part-time secretary, combined with a part-time salesperson position and part-time animal caregiver at a zoo.

Going overseas

You could also look for a suitable job abroad, in other words the rest of this big world. In the first place, look for countries where the economy is still growing, so new jobs are being created. Norway is such a country: thinly populated, swimming in oil and a language that is the easiest of all Scandinavian languages.

Before you sign a contract over the border, be aware that the protection that EU citizens enjoy is much stronger than outside the EU. Don't forget that you may need a visa and a work permit, and get information about the necessary insurance policies.

PS: The *cost of living* in the new country may be so high that your seemingly high salary melts like snow on a warm summer day.

Foreign aid and development work

A whole different ballgame is looking into foreign aid and development work, euphemistically called international cooperation. Africa and Latin America are the most sought after places. If you want to teach in these areas, that is always welcome. It will mostly pay little or nothing, but it will keep you fed. You get valuable life experience which certainly will not look bad on your CV.

Re-training

If you want to re-trained, it is important to find out where to look for a suitable position. In some cases, if there is a lot of demand in a certain industry, you may get a job offer right away – and the appropriate training will be paid by the employer or a board's study funds. You will have to figure out if you attracted to the work and can do it. And just as important: what will it mean for your further career? Will it ever be possible to return to the profession which you would prefer to stay in? (From medical sales representative to city bus driver.) Often this path will be blocked for good.

Studying

If jobhunting does not go well, it may be an option to begin a (new) study. You temporarily leave the workforce and hope to be able to take the next step 're-born', with a new diploma in your pocket. You shelter yourself from the economic rain and reappear when the sun starts shining again – putting off the execution. Don't worry about the study expenses. That is often a cheap excuse for doing nothing. 'No time' may also not be used as an excuse: you have enough time, but maybe you have to spend it more efficiently. (The busiest chaps learn a foreign language while being stuck in the traffic jam every day.)

Consider a university study (perhaps by the Open University), a college study (part-time or not) or an MBA course (via distant learning or not). There is a jungle full of training institutions where you can learn a language, management principles and skills, the ins and outs of certain software – you name it. Look for a study which expects a future sunny labour market and one which you are truly interested in. If not, you will probably quit before you finish or you will be educated 'for nothing'.

After you have made a choice, it is time to consider the financial side. Perhaps the costs are not that bad and you can finance the study yourself. If not, take out a bank loan, or from someone in your family. By the way, many institutions let you pay in instalments. And if they don't offer that, what prevents you from asking them? If you have earned an income, the taxman may give you a break (afterwards). Investigate the conditions. Turn your words into action!

Headhunters: the sequel

Waiting...waiting...waiting... for that telephone call that may never come is not the smartest approach. Make a regular tour of the headhunters or recruitment and selection agencies and let them know that you are still looking for this or that position. Even better, add a piece of news about yourself: an article by (or about) you from a professional magazine, a book review which you have written, the club's board which you are now a member of, the seminar that you gave, the study that you have just begun, the diploma that you have recently received, the congress at which you were invited to speak – be creative!

Maybe you do get an unexpected telephone call... The headhunter as an insurance policy.

Becoming your own boss

Another option you have is to work for yourself, which sometimes means: **creating** work. The freedom offered is very tempting, but what is the daily reality? Mostly, a lot of hard work and by definition, taking risks. Don't start up your own business because of a bitter feeling that you have towards an ex-boss and want to prove that your dismissal was a complete mistake. That motivation is paper thin.

Do you think you are made of the right entrepreneurial stuff?

- What proof do you have that entrepreneurial blood is flowing through your veins?
- Which entrepreneurial qualities do you have?
- One kind of entrepreneur is an all rounder, he can do everything. Are you that type of person?
- Another kind of entrepreneur has one specialism. Which one is yours?
- The third kind of entrepreneur is the salesperson. (The actual product is less relevant.) Is your strength being able to sell refrigerators to Eskimos and oil to the Saudis?
- Have you discovered a niche in the market? (What proof do you have?)
- Do you have enough money for working capital and to tide you over, without having to eat spaghetti every day?
- Are you a born optimist? Do you have strong self-discipline? Are you a 'self-starter'?

Write a business plan

If you are still seriously considering starting your own business, then there is a litmus test: write the business plan! (Banks and the Chamber of Commerce can give you an appropriate model, in paper or digital form.) What's more, you will have to produce a cash flow projection and a marketing plan. Experience shows that these activities scare off many people, because they will be confronted with the facts, the hard truth. Do you still want to go ahead? Put together the kind of plan that allows you to obtain a generous line of credit from the bank.

Summary

Main points

1. If you want to negotiate a better salary (you don't have to), take the initiative and prepare yourself well. (The boss will do that too.)
2. The employer's proposed agreement is the beginning of the negotiations, not the end.
3. You can fight for a lot of benefits, but what counts is the total package you end up with.
4. Within the law, there are many kinds of employment contracts; study the important details such as the non-competition clause.
5. Develop a plan B ahead of time, in case you still cannot find a suitable job. You could consider working abroad, re-training, going back to school or becoming your own boss.

Worthwhile websites

Thisismoney.co.uk	All about taxes and other money matters
Wageindicator.org	Salary information and checks (international)
Businessballs.com	Information about negotiations and other useful information
Negotiations.com	About Principled Negotiations
Startups.co.uk	For (future) entrepreneur

USEFUL WEBSITES

123tests.com
192.com
Allthejobs.co.uk
Aperfectcv.co.uk
Bestjobs.co.uk
Bsp.org.uk
Businessballs.com
Careerbuilder.co.uk
Careerjet.co.uk
Careers.ed.ac.uk
Cipd.co.uk
Coursesplus.co.uk
Direct.gov.uk/en/Employment/Jobseekers
Freelancers.net
Governmentjobsdirect.co.uk
Iacpr.org
Jobrapido.co.uk
Jobs.startpage.co.uk
Jobsearch.about.com
Learn.geek/interview.com
Lge.gov.uk
Mbaplaza.eu
Monster.co.uk
Negotiations.com
Prospects.ac.uk
Resume-resource.com
Sentient-recruitment.com
Shl.com
Startups.co.uk
Stepstone.com
Timeshighereducation.co.uk

Thisismoney.co.uk
Ukkey.co.uk
Wageindicator.org
Wfs.org
Workthing.com

INDEX

AC. *See* Assessment centre
Achievements, 106
Added value, 134
Administer, 117
Advertising yourself, 83
Age discrimination, 131
Agreements
  conditional, 181
Ambition, 36
Application letter
  checklist, 98
  design, 93
  example, 102, 105
  follow-up, 104
  letter of motivation, 94
  open, 94
  registering at an agency, 97
  types of, 93
Assessment centre
  competencies, 166
Assessment, 145, 158
Assessment centre, 161
  assignments, 164
  behavioural dimensions, 164
  determining potential, 162
  disqualifiers, 167
  exercises, 162
  meta dimensions, 164
Attachments, 49

Becoming an entrepreneur, 185
Behavioural dimensions, 164
Benefits, 171
Benefits statement plan, 179
Business plan, 185
Business sectors, 34

Career advice, 37
Career choice tests, 38
Career development, 37
Career statement, 49
Carry Out, 145
Chamber of commerce, 34
Company culture, 35
Company sites, 72
Compensation, 174
Competencies, 31, 106, 164, 166
Competitive advantage, 133
Conditional agreements, 181
Conditions of employment, 34
Contact moments
  creating, 107, 133
Contract, 171, 178
  alternative, 84
  flexi-work, 180
  freelance, 84
Creativity, 36
Curriculum vitae. *See* CV

CV, 27
  adapting, 51
  anonymity on, 47
  attachments, 49
  does it fit the job
    requirements?, 91
  dynamic, 41
  email address, 48
  evidence, 52
  example, 44
  functional, 41
  grades, 50
  inspiring, 52
  internships, 47
  key words, 51
  omissions, 47
  original, 50
  passport photo, 50
  Personal profile, 49
  reason for, 28
  reference to website or
    blog, 47
  references, 47
  registering on job sites, 70
  relevant experiences/skills,
    54
  striking, 50
  traditional chronological,
    40, 41
  types, 40
  writing, 40
CV-banks, 70

Day care, 176
Delay tactics, 18
Determining potential, 162

Development work, 183
Dismissal, 140
Disqualifiers, 167
Dress code, 131

Economic crisis
  changes during, 15
  competition in the labour
    market, 17
Educational possibilities, 175
Ego-research, 25
Elevator pitch, 108
Employer
  researching, 127
  suspicious, 90
Employment contracts, 178
E-test, 161
Ethics, 123
European Union
  working in, 84
Evidence portfolio, 118
Executive recruiter, 74
Exonomic crisis
  preventing redundancy, 17
Experience matrix, 120

Facebook, 71
Failure factors, 128
Field of study
  applying for a job outside,
    142
Flexibility, 180
Flexi-work, 180
Formulating goals, 19
Freelance contract, 84

Generalist, 32
Goals, 49
Grades, 50

Headhunters, 73, 184
  registering with, 97
High potential, 49, 54
Holidays, 175

Insurance, 175
Intelligence test, 158
Interim agencies, 80
Internship, 47
Internships, 82
Interview, 127, 145
  answering questions, 135
  asking questions, 136
  building blocks, 133, 140
  descriptive answers, 155
  exhibiting passion, 138
  first-minute, and last-
    minute, 153
  humour, 137
  language use, 148
  main points of, 151
  making a good impression,
    130
  orientation, 147
  pillars of, 150
  preparing for, 127
  presenting yourself as an
    interview partner, 155
  psychological, 167, 168
  researching the company,
    133
  STAR method, 139

starter's problems, 140
  tips, 156
  types of, 147
  types of questions, 152
  unexpected developments,
    138
  use of your voice, 137
  web, 150
  what to do after the ~, 133
  why questions, 147
Interview partners
  researching, 129
Investigate, 59

Job
  accepting any ~, 27
  looking for, 59
  proving suitability, 127
Job application
  open, 81, 94
Job centres. *See* Jobcentre
  Plus
Job description, 60
  example, 64
Job fairs, 83
Job hunting
  abroad, 84
  delay tactics, 18
  formulating goals, 19
  hurdles, 65
  maximising chances, 20
Job hunting codes, 123
Job interview. *See* Interview
Job portfolio, 182
Job sites, 67
Job titles, 60

Job vacancies
  hidden jobs, 73
  in newspapers and
    magazines, 73
  on company sites, 72
Job vacancy
  analysis, 61
  looking for, 59
  search schedule, 69
  sources, 66, 84
  suitable, 62, 91
  testing whether position
    demands are realistic, 60
  text, 62
  the biggest job bank, 81
  via headhunters, 73
  via internet, 67, 72
  via job fairs, 83
  via networking, 76
  via networks, 80
  via radio and tv, 82
  via recruitment and
    slection agencies, 73
  via temp agencies, 80
Jobcentre Plus, 81
Job-hopping, 28
Jobs
  hidden, 73
  overseas, 182
  part-time, 182

Key words, 51
KIRAP-CS
  job hunting steps, 19
Knowing, 27

Knowledge
  transferable, 32

Labour agreements, 173
Labour market
  competition, 17
Language use, 148
Lease car, 174
Letter of application
  sending regularly, 89
Letter of motivation, 94
  reaction to a tip, 97
  traditional, 95
LinkedIn, 71
Lowering the risks, 143

Magazines
  vacancies in, 73
Management tests, 160
Maximising chances, 20
Mega job sites, 68
Meta dimensions, 164
Motivation, 138
MySpace, 71
Network
  social, 39, 71

Networking, 76
Networks, 80
  goal-oriented networking,
    79
  primary, 78
  secondary, 78
  social, 72
  which relationships do you
    make use of?, 77

Newspapers
   vacancies in, 73
Non-competition clause, 180

Orientation interview, 147
Outplacement, 179
Overqualified, 114
Overseas jobs, 182
Oversees jobs, 84
Overtime, 175

Part-time jobs, 182
Pension, 175
Performance review, 179
Personality profile, 29
Personality test, 159
Practice, 84
Prepare, 127
Profession
   meaning of, 39
Profile sketch, 27
Profit-sharing, 175
Progress report, 21
Proving suitability, 127
Psychological interview, 167
Psychological test, 158

Questionnaires, 52
Questions
   answering, 135
   asking, 136
   progress ~, 137
   types of, 152
   why ~, 147

Radio commercials, 82

React, 89
Reaction
   no ~ to a letter, 124
Reasons for leaving, 154
Recruitment and selection
   agencies, 73
Recruitment and selection
   agency, 184
   registering with, 97
Re-entrants, 52
   relevant experience/skills,
   54
References, 47, 121
Rejection
   dealing with, 22, 115, 124,
   158
Resumé, 28
Re-training, 183

Salary
   and taxation, 178
   breakdown, 176
   components, 174
   determining size of, 177
   negotiating, 171
   principled negotiations,
   177
Savings plans, 175
Sector, 33
Selection agency
   psychological, 168
Self-analysis, 29
   tunnel vision, 29
   what can I do?, 31
   what do I want?, 33
   who am I?, 30

Self-knowledge, 27
Self-reflection, 22
Sign the Contract, 171
Skills, 31
  transferable, 32
Social networks, 39, 71, 72
Specialist, 32
STAR method, 139
Starter, 52, 140
  applying for a job outside
    your field of study, 142
  battle against experiences
    competitors, 142
  long period of
    unemployment, 141
  relevant experience/skills,
    55
  relevant experiences/skills,
    54
  specific problems, 140
Studying, 183

Talents, 31
Telephone script, 110
Telephone tips, 113
Telephone-phobia, 110

Temp agencies, 80
Test
  case study, 168
  e~, 161
  intelligence, 158
  management, 160
  personality, 159
  psychological, 158
Thirteenth month, 175
Trade journals
  vacancies in, 73
Tunnel vision, 29
Tv commercials, 82
Twitter, 71

Unemployment, 13
  job hunting after a period
    of, 141
Unique selling points (USP),
  35

Web interview, 150
Weekly activity scheme, 122
Why questions, 147
Work experience, 31
  none or too little, 56